THE JOY OF SUMO

THE JOY OF
SUMO
A Fan's Notes

DAVID BENJAMIN
illustrations by Greg Holfeld

Published by the Charles E. Tuttle Company, Inc.
of Rutland, Vermont & Tokyo, Japan
with editorial offices
2-6 Suido 1-chome, Bunkyo-ku, Tokyo 112

LCC Card No. 91-65047
ISBN 0-8048-1679-3

First edition, 1991
Third printing, 1993

CHARLES E. TUTTLE COMPANY
Rutland, Vermont & Tokyo, Japan

Printed in Japan

Published by the Charles E. Tuttle Company, Inc.
of Rutland, Vermont & Tokyo, Japan
with editorial offices at
2-6 Suido 1-chome, Bunkyo-ku, Tokyo 112

LCC Card No. 91-65057
ISBN 0-8048-1679-4

First edition, 1991
Third printing, 1992

Printed in Japan

for Annie & Swede

CONTENTS

ACKNOWLEDGMENTS

Even a book written in paranoid seclusion requires a little help from one's friends. I derived, for example, a certain measure of residual inspiration from a handful of friends who always said it could be done: Alice Twombly, Linda Flashinski, Jill Ramsfield, Bill Breen, and two former mentors at Beloit College, Alan Perles and Denny Moore. I also credit three guys I've never met, Bil Gilbert, Leigh Montville and William Goldman—who've proven that sportswriting can be beautiful.

For inspiration plus insight, my wife, Junko Yoshida, is the mother lode.

Former colleagues at *Tokyo Journal*, Anthony J. Bryant and Margaret Ng, helped birth this book, which was originally a feature article called "The Joy of Sumo." And it was Margaret who helped me pursue, across several continents, the best illustrator I've ever worked with, Greg Holfeld. Terry Lloyd and Tomomi Okawara at Linc Computer (not to mention Roger the Conversion King) saved this ms. at its darkest hour, when I discovered I had written it in a computer dialect that is unknown outside the lost continent of Atlantis.

Too many editors took a pass at this book, but the considerate ones were Tuttle editorial directors Ray Furse and Philip Sandoz, and the useful ones were Kim Schuefftan and Dave Russell. Also, a nod to Mark Schilling, who circulates among sumo nerds, for giving me invaluable insight into their tortured psyches.

INTRODUCTION

"Well, it's kind of interesting, but they're so fa-a-at!"

Every real fan creates his sport in his own image.

Me, I'm a sumo fan. Been that way since 1987. Long time. And what's sumo to me?

Well, it's ballet and it's bullfighting . . .

—blundering and grace . . .

—dignity and buffoonery . . .

—lightning and molasses . . .

—suet and gristle . . .

—the monstrous and the minuscule . . .

—the loner and the mob.

It's choreography and spontaneity . . .

—honor and corruption . . .
—the cerebral and the Neanderthal . . .
—basketball and judo . . .
—football and the balance beam.
It's frogs and princes . . .
—clerics and clowns . . .
—Brer Rabbit and Brer Bear . . .
—d'Artagnan and Quasimodo . . .
—silk and mud . . .
—tits and ass . . .
—incense and beer.

Sumo is, minute for minute, split second for split second, the best sport in the world to watch. It's sudden and violent. Almost no rules. One guy against the other and the ref (most of the time) is just another pretty pair of pajamas.

And sumo—no question—is the best sport there is if you're prone to imagine yourself in there, swinging away—because all these guys are out of shape . . .

• because you've got little guys going up against humongous guys—and winning! . . .

• because fat guys take on guys who look like Schwarzenegger, and beat 'em! . . .

• because women pour out of the bleachers to touch you! (So what if they're all 50 years old? They're women!)

Sumo is a splendid sport, a joy to discover, a fascination to pursue. I came to it as a sports fan—one of the last dinosaurs who still admits that I like watching it at least as much as I enjoy "feeling the burn." And it is from that point of view that I write this book. I know well that many others, especially gaijin (foreigners), come to sumo from a perspective which, although I often deplore it, is equally fertile.

They, among others, see sumo as a Cultural Treasure of Japan.

I remember when I met Doreen Simmons, the reigning queen of gaijin sumo experts in Tokyo. I told her I was writing a sumo book and she fixed on me a suspicious and proprietary squint. What sort of book? she wanted to know.

"Well, from the point of view of the sports fan."

Doreen smiled with relief and lowered her deflector shields. "Well," she said, "I don't care about *that.*"

Sumo is the only sport in the world in which the foremost expert need not know, or care, about what happens among the athletes on the field. Imagine a book about the World Cup in which the road to the championship is a mere backdrop for discussions, in much finer detail, of Ruud Gullit's household habits and meal schedule, or Gianluca Vialli's favorite pasta shape.

But in sumo, this is the norm. Much of the interest, among foreigners, dwells on a tiny, weird backstage domain, a cloister, "the sumo world," in which its participants circulate—bedtimes, hairdos, hobbies, medical history, marital aids . . .

I have begun to suspect that this unnatural focus on background—rather than competition—plays a major role in the odd, and grotesque, image of sumo outside Japan. To me, before I began to see sumo as a sport, and not such a weird sport at that, it was half Oriental mystery, half disgusting joke. I've noticed that this is how most gaijin view it.

But wait! This isn't just a gaijin prejudice. Japanese people, because they live here, don't feel obligated to revere sumo as a cultural tabernacle—which means they apply entirely private and arbitrary (read: "normal") criteria, when they're kids, to decide whether they really enjoy watching fat men grab each other's love handles and do the lambada.

Yeah, even in Japan, sumo—like pickled plums, noodle-slurping and urinating in public (all popular facets of Japanese culture)—is an acquired taste. Among most Japanese, a fondness for sumo grows slowly in the reluctant psyche—which explains why the average age of a sumo crowd at the Ryogoku Kokugikan (Tokyo's national sumo arena) is nearer fifty years than twenty.

Reiko Komiya, a housewife of my acquaintance and a woman of vehement opinion, typifies sumo's acceptance problem among even the natives. When she was a young girl in Niigata, there was no television. Sumo wrestlers were disembodied radio heroes. Reiko's favorite was Akinoumi, arch-rival to the immortal Futabayama.

For years, she crouched beside the crystal set and followed the trials of Akinoumi like Addie Pray enthralled by Fibber McGee. And then, a miracle. Her parents took Reiko, just then becoming a teenager, to Tokyo to see her sumo idols in the flesh. But . . .

Oops. Too much flesh. "I was so disappointed," she said, her face still—almost 50 years later—reflecting that moment of disillusionment. "They were so fa-at." Reiko, since, has recovered her affection, but only after a long interval of apostasy.

Western observers, bred in cultures where "you can never be too rich or too thin," share Reiko's childhood antipathy, and complicate it with the suspicion that there is something vaguely obscene in the brief glimpses of sumo that seep now and then through the chrysanthemum curtain. Phidias and

D.H. Lawrence both gave us graphic depictions of young men entwined in combat, but ah, these striplings were lissom, chaste, and handsome—unsullied (except in the prurient mind) by even the vaguest intimation of, well . . .

Hush, it is unspoken. We are forbidden to suggest it, lest we invite the wrath of sumo's purists. But it lurks, anyway, in the backs of our minds. Naked men. With breasts. Jiggling. Embracing. Touching one another . . .

Remember. For most of us foreigners, what was the first sumo we ever saw? Those old Movietone news clips from Japan, right? It seemed like the camera angle was always the same. You were sitting there in the Bijou suddenly looking up at the world's biggest ass—fish-belly white, with these wormy bands of cellulite and little red pimply flecks. And the only consolation was that the worst part—the middle—was (barely) covered with . . . Jesus, what is that? A diaper?

And then this immense tochis—you remember?—to which was attached Jabba the Hutt, flung itself forward into a similar mutant. Here's where you noticed they both had these short pudgy arms, and they started to grope at each other, like manatees in heat . . .

And that's where the clip always ended, probably because it was unfit for family viewing. God, what if they ripped off each other's diapers?

Well, those are great memories—and hard ones to erase. But there's more to sumo (thank God) than this weird vision of two gay lumberjacks undressing each other in a sandbox. That, after all, is a fleeting misperception. So forget it. See sumo, instead, as

tim—that of all beside it conveys such simplicity
and innocence.
this kid stuff.

I can't think of a sport more childish than sumo.
When you're a sumo wrestler, you get to live in a
clubhouse, where no "girls" are allowed. You're
encouraged to eat all you want and have "thirds" on
dessert, nap all afternoon, and drink beer all night.
When you play, you get to halfway to build mud and
roll in the dirt. And a whole match? It rarely lasts
more than 10 seconds, so you're not late for
dinner. You never have guests to the room, or sweat
or the hot sun. You never have to think about what's
good for the "team", and as long as you keep building
bigger and fatter, you don't even have to pay
attention to their diet.

Sumo is the only sport I can think of that allows you
to be a superstar and a couch potato at the same
time—which, of course, creates some striking affinity
between the jerk on the TV couch and the slob
sitting in front of it. Y see? Sumo isn't just for the
heavyset!

"Sure", you say, "but if only they weren't so fat—"

Why, it's exactly here that we come back to contemplate
those things I love most of sumo's "majesty". Well,
because in a fatness—it is sumo's life-hoarded molar),
its drawback itself—that is to say, its obesity/muscle is
to hoard it...more into microscopic... as it is
to hoard it... its sluggish proportion of its very simpler
and likes Tatum to prove all—it is Heath itself to
be/one. As you learn to live with it, you come oddly to
appreciate it, but only with a conscious effort.

fun—first of all because it conveys such simplicity and innocence.

It's kid stuff.

I can't think of a sport more childish than sumo. When you're a sumo wrestler, you get to live in a clubhouse where no girls are allowed. You're encouraged to eat all you want and have "thirds" on dessert, nap all afternoon, and drink beer all night. When you play, you get to take off all your clothes and roll in the dirt. And a whole match hardly ever takes more than 10 seconds; so you're never late for dinner. You never have games in the rain, the snow, or the hot sun. You never have to think about what's good for the "team," and as long as you keep getting bigger and fatter, you don't even have to pay attention to the coach.

Sumo is the only sport in the world that allows you to be a superstar and a couch potato at the same time—which, of course, creates a magical affinity between the jock on the TV screen and the slob sitting in front of it. Y'see? Sumo isn't just fun. It's hog heaven!

"Sure," you say, "but if only they weren't so fa-at . . ."

Why do people keep coming back to contemplate those flanks of blubber—staring, judging? Well, because it's there. Fat is sumo's two-headed nickel, its draw and its flaw. Fat is to sumo as chin music is to baseball . . . as the offsides rule to soccer . . . as race is to basketball . . . as the specter of Darryl Stingley and Jack Tatum to pro football . . . as Death itself to boxing. As you learn to live with it, you come oddly to appreciate it, but only with a conscious effort.

Try to get this into your head. This isn't your

aerobics class. This is Japan, where the fat and the sylphlike, the whale and the butterfly, Audrey Hepburn and Meat Loaf, share the same aesthetic universe and coexist in perfect harmony. The Japanese see little dissonance in aesthetic paradox, which is why a sumo wrestler usually marries a woman no larger than his right thigh.

Fortunately, there are three ways to overcome the irrational anti-fat (and secretly homophobic) bias that prevents the full, idiotic enjoyment of sumo. These are as follows:

1) THINK Japanese. Unlike Westerners, Japanese tend not to fret if a little boy goes through his formative years eating like a septic tank and swelling up like a corn-fed stoat. Remember that this is an island nation whose Depression started two years early, in 1927, and lapped right over into more than ten years of wartime austerity, which was followed by a postwar famine that consumed another decade. These people starved for 40 years.

So, let's hear it for fat boys, the showpieces of the Japanese economic miracle. "Things are looking up, Hiroshi! There goes another kid who looks like the Michelin tire man."

2) BECOME Japanese. The sumo world, according to popular legend, is a closed world, unchanged for centuries. Its intricacies, unfathomable to the outsider, are a lens to peer into the mystery that is Japan. But to behold Japan through this pinhole, you must learn Japanese and then master the special patois of sumo, throw yourself into research and memorize lists of the great wrestlers and champions of the past. Introduce yourself to *oyakata*

(stable masters) and attend practices. Meet the wrestlers, ingratiate yourself with the Sumo Association, wangle yourself a free pass to all the *basho* (tournaments), immerse yourself in the private lives, the gossip, the scandals, the daily routine, the emotional burdens, and the physical discomforts of the sumo wrestlers.

This is, of course, more exertion than most employed people have time for, and it poses the danger that you'll become more Japanese than the Japanese—thus rendering yourself offensive to everyone, regardless of race, color, or national origin.

Nevertheless, there is a surprisingly large group of foreigners in Japan (commonly known as sumo nerds) who have taken this vicarious route to enlightenment.

3) OSMOSIS, or casual exposure, is a more felicitous way to learn sumo's delights. This method's most endearing feature is that it doesn't require you to be Japanese or to go native. Any gaijin who spends more than a few weeks in Japan inevitably notices little flashes of sumo popping up in daily life. In the morning on the subway, he sees sumo photos in sports tabloids and weekly magazines. You'll probably notice *Japan Times'* English coverage of each basho, usually written by the inimitable Andy Adams. TV provides sumo highlights on the news, and "Sumo Digest" every night (during a basho) on TV Asahi. You might even flip through a copy of Adams' magazine, *Sumo World,* if it turns up in someone's bathroom library.

And then, there are the *rikishi* (wrestlers) themselves. You encounter them on the street. They're not like Western athletes, who either avoid public contact or go out only in disguise. Sumo wrestlers are obvious. Decked out in their official garb of bathrobe and shower thongs, they roam the streets of Tokyo like ambulatory roadblocks, foraging in the daytime for *chankonabe* (their favorite food) and at night for nookie (their favorite pastime).

But by far the average person's most likely exposure to sumo is NHK-TV. The basho are held six times a year (in all the odd-numbered months), and the national television network broadcasts not only every one, but the whole thing, from wire to wire, for 15 days, including weekends—with no commercial interruptions. Faced with this year-round sumo explosion on Japan's most important TV source, the average channel-hopper usually ends up seeing quite a bit of sumo whether he had planned to or not. And he notices gradually that he is becoming inured to those physical anomalies of the sumo wrestler that once seemed so repellent.

In these repeated glimpses, unsightly fat becomes mere physical bulk, the necessary armor of battle between giants. At the same time, the rikishi, who seem at first to be indistinguishable larger-than-life Japanese archetypes, evolve into smaller, more likeable creatures: individuals, odd characters, regular guys. Heroes, even. As this happens, curiosity plants its seed, and the passion—especially among those already initiated aficionados of the ring, the mat, the gridiron or the rink—grows!

If you, too, have ever felt this tingle of sumo curiosity, then this book is for you.

But heed this warning. If you regard sumo not as a sport—to watch and to cheer, to handicap and bet on, to shout for your favorites, and hiss your personal villains—then perhaps you'd be happier with a do-it-yourself rock gardening manual. In any case, skip this book. There are many volumes that perpetuate the stuffy image of sumo preferred by its traditionalists (who dominate the Sumo Association). In this book, I have intentionally violated the conventional approaches to sumo that seem especially cherished by the fraternity of gaijin groupies.

Sumo, for example, began as a form of gladiatorial entertainment to amuse the captive royal court in Kyoto, and assumed a measure of seriousness by mimicking Shinto religious ritual. Essentially, it began its history as a trashsport—no more credible or significant than its present-day parallels—ice dancing, professional wrestling, synchronized swimming, demolition derby, et cetera. Sumo, however, matured long ago into legitimacy. The wrestlers became genuine athletes whose foremost interest is not to appear picturesque, ridiculous or cute, but to win—and by their efforts thus to (a) make a living and, (b) entertain the spectators. Some institutions, unwritten strictures and traditions in sumo hinder this private drive. These bureaucratic intrusions prevail despite—not because of—the competitors' commitment to their job.

Moreover, I think it unfair to sumo to treat it merely as a cultural pageant. This approach represents an essentially impractical form of fanhood. It's possible to delight in ritual throughout one whole day of sumo, and maybe even 36 hours, but no more. If, after watching 20 or more bouts, you haven't grasped the intense drama of each confrontation, or discovered the special style of even one rikishi, you will soon weary of culture and go back to your Mickey Spillane.

This book is for fans, or folks who want to be fans. The game is the thing; it's the joy of sumo. All the showbiz, and cultural trappings—whether they're pretty, or strange, or funny, or just plain tedious— fade into insignificance once two rikishi face each other across the ring.

Like just about every other good spectator sport, sumo is fun because you can ignore the buildup, publicity, post-mortem analyses and the prejudices of your fellow fans, and just watch. The more you watch, the more you know and the less you need to depend on self-appointed experts (like me) to tell you whether we're having fun yet.

Herein, then, is freedom from expert opinion! I will guide the casual but astute fan through the stages of sumophilia. We will go from ignorance to obsession, but we'll stick mainly to those aspects of sumo that emerge inevitably from seeing it on TV—or, if you must, Movietone News.

If this approach seems personal, it is. This is how I learned sumo, by myself in the privacy of my own rabbit hutch, and I think it's the best way.

Come on along.

THE PIT

The typical sumo novice gets his first taste of the sport in one of two ways. Mine came at home, where I spend my days writing. I turned to NHK's sumo broadcasts as respite from work and from the vast wasteland of Japanese daytime TV. I wasn't eager to watch fat guys with greasy hairdos mauling each other in public, but after six hours of staring at a word processor screen, even sumo is a welcome respite.

Such chance encounters on the boob tube have spawned a legion of gaijin (foreign) sumophiles and at least one J (Japanese) fan: my wife Junko, who, before my influence, ranked sumo on her list of "Favorite Things To Do" just above a Novocaine injection to the roof of her mouth. However, I'm afraid more people discover sumo the other way, which is when some culture vulture hauls you down to the Ryogoku Kokugikan (go ahead, try to say that three times fast) to see the waltzing whales in the flesh. This is not the ideal first encounter with sumo, although I do recommend periodic visits to the Kokugikan to keep yourself in touch with all the smells and sensations and noises of sumo. If Ryogoku is your first full dose of sumo (without a session or two of TV orientation), you're in danger of being grossed out—as Reiko Komiya was—or suffering cultural overload.

At the arena, at first blush, the ring is not the thing. Look around. If you bought the affordable seats in the upper deck, you have a great vantage point to drink in the spectacle spread out before you. The crowd, which arrives gradually, wanders and visits, and chatters endlessly. The crowd is the aspect of sumo that television cannot convey. A day at the sumo basho is Japan's Chautauqua; town meeting time; the parish pancake breakfast.

Ushers, dressed in ancient costumes whose sleeves drape almost to the floor, shuffle constantly, guiding spectators, serving beverages and piles of food to the fans in the high-priced box seats that circle the sandbox (*dohyo*, actually). Food is incessant at the sumo matches. And expensive.

Traditionally (every explanation in sumo begins with the word, "traditionally"), the box seats are "owned," managed and doled out by teahouses. In order for me to occupy a box seat for one day's sumo, for example, my wife made a connection with a fellow worker from Shitamachi (the old, picturesque part of

Tokyo). Her neighbor was a second- or third-generation member of the "support group" for the Dewanoumi *sumobeya* (sumo stable), which is, of course, affiliated with a certain Tokyo teahouse.

(If you're not keeping up with all this, don't worry. Sumo, like many things Japanese, is swollen with arcana that transfix gaijin and paralyze them with awestruck absorption. The Japanese, who prefer to use sumo for day-to-day amusement, tend to bypass such bullshit and go straight to the good stuff.)

For one box, which holds four Japanese-size people, the price is a cool ¥100,000 (about $750.). For that, you are treated to enough food to keep you bloated for the next 48 hours, and as much beer, sake or whiskey as you can fit into the box among your legs, bags, coats, umbrellas and gifts.

Gifts? If this is Japan, there must be *omiyage!* To show their gratitude for your purchase of the tickets, the teahouse unloads into your laps four shopping bags, stuffed with sumo souvenirs—most of it food and most of it yummy (if you only had an appetite left!). These gifts compete for space with you, your personal effects, the growing accumulation of empty bottles, used *yakitori* sticks, half-consumed *obento* (box lunches) and other flotsam. Just about the time you begin to feel your first pangs of claustrophobia, oop! Hey! It's over—perfectly timed! The last match arrives at the same moment, it seems, when you couldn't endure—for even ten more minutes—sitting there, cross-legged, holding yourself erect and supporting the slumped form of the old man in the next box who has polished off his tenth bottle of Asahi Super Dry and fallen noisily asleep on your shoulder.

If the idea of strangers falling asleep on your shoulder bothers you, you shouldn't be in Japan. But, even if you didn't manage a box seat and didn't collect three or four cubic meters of omiyage and the person next to you stays awake, there is still plenty of atmosphere at the arena to distract you from the actual sumo.

Lean over the upper deck railing and scan. The box seats and "sand seats" close to the dohyo are a mosaic of aging Japanese. Very few children. You might spot (the NHK cameramen always do) a few young women, who've come as guests of an aunt or uncle. There are always several uncomfortable, squished-looking gaijin businessmen in rumpled suits. But mostly, this is an *obaa-san/ojii-san* (Grandma and Gramps) occasion. The obaa-san tend to be overdressed in their brightest frocks and beaded sweaters. The ojii-san are slightly underdressed in baggy pants, tweed coats and knit shirts; they look like horseplayers hanging around the paddock (and most of them, on other days, are).

Listen to the constant buzz, the bursts of ladies' laughter and the bark of masculine grunting (Japanese men speak in the manliest male argot this side of Texas), and you might—if you shut your eyes—imagine that you've come upon an enormous combined Tupperware Party and Lions Club convention. Many of these people come for the sumo, but many don't know sumo nearly as well as the TV fan watching at home. This is a once-a-year social occasion, a pretext for friends and relatives to gather at one place, eat, drink, and jabber. In Tokyo, which is a city of incessant and almost painful tension, the Ryogoku Kokugikan is one of the few truly leisurely scenes you will ever witness. The old man who falls asleep halfway through the wrestling or turns to his companion to say, "When does Wakanohana (who retired in 1983) wrestle?" is an integral part of the experience in Ryogoku—where the January, May, and September basho occur—or in Osaka in March, Nagoya in July, Fukuoka in November.

Sumo is a 15-day picnic six times a year, and the sports just happen to be part of it—for many, an insignificant part.

After you've drunk all this in, and it doesn't take long, you haven't really missed much of the action. Down there. On the dohyo. Way down there. (Opera glasses are a popular accessory at the sumo matches.) As you peer down at that small, brightly lit mound of dried mud and sand, you should feel a tingle of recognition—I mean, if you (like me) are really a Fan, and not just a voyeur sopping up one more facet of Oriental mystery.

A word should pop into your mind, a word that hearkens back to high school sports. You recognize this arena for what it is. This is a pit!

"Death Valley"

In modern sports, certainly at the professional level, pits have become almost extinct. Certain stadiums, like "Death Valley" in Clemson, South Carolina, or Soldiers Field in Chicago, or Boston Garden during the NBA playoffs, or "The Pit" itself, the old basketball court at the University of New Mexico, sometimes earn the label, but they are only a mild facsimile. A real pit is where the only dividing line between fans and players is a wall of flesh and a thin veneer of self-restraint. A pit is a place where fans breathe on the players and the players spray sweat onto the throng. A pit is where fans and players are so close that they stand knee-deep in the same pool of emotion and feed each other with anger, fear, outrage and exultation. A pit smells, feels, looks, and roars like a figment of Dante's imagination.

All right, admittedly, the Ryogoku Kokugikan presents no such infernal terrors. Everybody loves the sumo wrestlers. But in shape and atmosphere, this is a pit. No other major sports arena in the world seats its fans right up to the edge, the sideline, the brink of the playing field. A look down above the dohyo is a wondrous sight. The sand of the dohyo is dazzling under the TV lights. The ring or *tawara* is a circle (made of rice bales) inside a square. The edge of the square drops off precipitously to a narrow aisle— and beyond that, in all directions, people. Every day, sumo wrestlers fly off the dohyo—250, 300, 400, 500 pounds of hurtling blubber—into the laps of the fans.

And how do the fans react? They laugh, they hoot! They slap the careening monsters on the shoulders and mop the sweat from their clothes. There is no dividing line. Wrestlers coming and going shoulder their way through spectators who clog the aisles to pat their backs and exult in their proximity. Sumo is a pit sport, and this place, the Ryogoku Kokugikan, is the ultimate, perfectly symmetrical, klieg-lit, high-tech, air-conditioned Pit. If there is a better sports arena, more ideally suited for the texture and emotion of its sport, it is not on this planet.

Rhythm and Recognition

You appreciate this atmosphere, and if you're a veteran fan, you let it infect you...and then, eventually, you notice the sumo itself. The essence of watching sumo, properly, is its rhythm. A day's sumo moves to its own beat, and you feel the beat best only when you're at the Pit.

Second best (and very close), is the NHK live broadcast every day, which follows the action from start to finish, saturates the viewer with instant replay and never breaks the mood with beer commercials.

For those whose jobs do not allow them a two-week vacation six times a year to follow the basho, there is a nightly wrap-up show on TV Asahi, called "Sumo Digest." I only watch it as a last resort because it reduces the more than six hours of sumo to a 30-minute highlight reel. All you see is the main matches of the day, none of the Class A, and B, and C matches. None of the circling and pawing and scowling. Just the clash, the struggle and the fall. It's like watching a baseball wrap-up on the 11 o'clock news. All those homers, but not a single hit-and-run—that ain't baseball, Mel!

Sumo is a stalking dance, and the stalking begins early in the day, with the lower level—*makushita*—wrestlers, the kids in dull brown belts. Makushita matches are rushed. They last little longer than a "Sumo Digest" highlight clip. And the ritual chest-thumping that characterizes sumo is forbidden among the scrubs. But they are part of the beat. The stalking dance whispers its rhythm first in makushita.

As the wrestling progresses upward into the higher makushita divisions, the matches lengthen, the dance slows. And the audience feels the deepening gravity of the drama on the dohyo. There are two upper divisions in sumo, *makuuchi* (the top) and *juryo.* In soccer, the equivalent would be first and second division; in baseball, the Majors and Triple-A. Unlike baseball, though, the Majors in sumo divide up into further permutations. The official upper-division sumo ranks, starting from the exalted and proceeding downward, are: *yokozuna, ozeki, seki-wake, komusubi,* and *maegashira.*

The gangs of makuuchi and juryo wrestlers, respectively, start their matches with a parade. They wear bright belts (*mawashi*). They get to throw salt and drink holy water and spit. The matches slow down. The endless buzz of socializing fades momentarily when each clash finally erupts. And as the rhythm slows, as the matches become more important, and the tension builds, every seat in the arena fills, and the Pit falls dead silent when the monsters collide.

And for those of you watching at home, working or reading or munching, there are sudden moments of suspension. "Wait. *Jikan desu!* (It's time!)"

Without all the strutting and dawdling, glowering and posing, the extraordinary drama of sumo would boil down to fat men with dirty feet trying to push each other's noses into their brains. No other sport so effectively, so seductively glorifies itself in the midst of its own delivery. No other sport has sumo's melodramatic contrast of stasis and explosion. Baseball, another game of waiting, staring and posing, comes closest, perhaps, but never—like sumo—guarantees, even once, that desperate, decisive climax that happens more than 30 times in every day of sumo.

Foreplay, if you will, and orgasm.

Even to the newcomer, the atmosphere—mounting drama in the midst of a Golden Ager picnic—is the first, obvious charm of the sport. And it can seduce you into coming back—or, more economically, tuning in again. And again.

Then a deeper grip takes hold. As you sit there, faithfully feeding on the day's action in the sandbox, some of those formless dumplings become vaguely familiar. You notice shapes, hairlines, habits, tics. Tits. Asses. In all that pawing and groping, especially if you've been a fan of some sport sometime in your life, you begin to see patterns. And it occurs to you.

"Jesus Christ! These guys are using technique! These tubs have style!" Well, some of them do. Toyonoumi will never have a clue.

There! You see what happens? You start to learn their names!

But I get ahead of myself. You don't catch the names right away. The first day of sumo, either at the Pit or on the tube, is a blur. But if you were lucky that day, you were intrigued. You got used to the fat and decided that all these guys were not homosexual showoffs (And if so, what the hell? So was Rock Hudson). You enjoyed (or so you say) the rituals. You felt the beat, noticed the drama of sumo. You caught the first symptoms. The fever has begun to warp your pysche.

You might even be so fascinated after one day—or two—that you go out and Buy The Book. Sumo nerds all need to write The Book, their own definitive guide that sets the world straight on the Essence of Sumo. So there are plenty of sumo guides out there. They tend toward a numbing sameness but, nevertheless, are eventually necessary. The one I use is *Sumo: From Rite to Sport* by P.L. Cuyler (Weatherhill). Lora

Sharnoff's *Grand Sumo* (also Weatherhill) is said by some to be the new Revised Standard Bible of sumo, but it's expensive. The one universal feature of all the Books is how much of the information—slit, gutted and spread out in gory detail—is superfluous and pedantic. And boring. Which is why you should take my advice and don't read The Book before you catch the fever. Without passion, all sports lore is gibberish.

The game is the thing. Tune in. As you watch every afternoon on NHK, you'll find yourself studying the daily listings on the *Japan Times* sports pages. You try to remember their names.

KotoinazumaKitakachidokiKushimaumiKoboya-maKinishikiKotonishikiKasugafujiKyokuDOzanKyo-kuGOzan . . . Kee-rist!

It doesn't really work. But that's OK, because you start to recognize them in other ways. Little things pop up and give personality to the names (like Ted Kluszewski's bare arms, or Mickey Rivers flipping his bat after a swing-and-a-miss). Look. This one's cute. This one's unbelievably ugly. This one has a baby blue diaper. That one's losing his hair. And that one . . .

"God, who's *that*? He's sweating like a pig!"

BIG AL
and the Silver Spoons

Forget the sweaty one for a minute. He's unique, he's cute, he's funny. But he's a putz. He isn't gonna do it for you.

Y'see, you gotta connect.

In your first day of watching sumo, it's likely you will note almost nothing of the competitors themselves, especially if you're too far from the dohyo to notice how sweaty the sweaty one is. However, although the whole scene passes you by as just a sort of pinkish haze, you must awaken to at least one extraordinary wrestler. One hulk must catch your eye and fire your imagination.

Person-to-person. It's how you connect.

The one who did it to me was the one who, I

39

suspect, was the greatest of them all: Chiyonofuji. Chiyo, or "the Wolf" as the press liked to call him, retired in May of 1991. He was a wrestler who bore the unmistakable mark of immortality, like Pele or Julius Erving. He quietly forced the entire sumo galaxy to revolve around him. Other sumo wrestlers have recently begun to emulate his regimen, physique and style, but when I began to succumb to the pleasures of sumo back in 1987 there was no one even close to Chiyonofuji.

For one thing, he looked different. He had, f'rinstance, no boobs—just a smooth, granite slab of pectoral muscle. No jellied blankets of suet rippled beneath his skin. His belly, a small hard bulge above his belt, did not bounce like a cantaloupe in a nylon bag. His arms were not the elbowless sausages with baby-fists that seem obligatory among sumo wrestlers. His arms, really, were the striking feature of Chiyonofuji's aspect. They reminded me of the coal miners with whom I once worked, round-shouldered mountain men whose arms were a paradox of mass and dexterity. Such arms are not huge and distended like those on the denizens of Gold's Gym. But they are heavy—too heavy, certainly, to lift with a normal human shoulder—with bulges at forearm and bicep that never seem to relax, as though they'd been artfully packed with riverbed stones. Yet, such arms—coal-miner, Chiyonofuji arms—swing and flex with a feathery lightness. Chiyonofuji carried truncheons, but moved them like wings.

Chiyo, even without the usual indulgence one grants to the swollen face of the large athlete, was handsome. Not matinee-idol beautiful, but handsome. He affected none of the theatricality of lesser wrestlers; he was almost trancelike in his demeanor from the moment he entered the arena and bowed to the ring judges, to the instant of his victory when— suddenly—he betrayed himself as perhaps sumo's most expressive, emotional competitor.

One noticed Chiyonofuji, irresistibly, because in his face, his body, his skill, one could see the art and discipline of sumo. From the great artists of the sport, the fan begins to measure his own interest and define his attachment to sumo. He connects.

That connection happens only to sports fans. If it doesn't happen, you never become a sports fan, and you don't understand why some people do. Even among fans, there are vast gulfs of incomprehension, because one human heart has only enough room for a few such passions. The sports with which you don't connect become, at best, alien pastimes. At worst, they are the enemy of sport itself, squandering great athletes, precious natural resources, and valuable air time.

I don't think anyone is immune from the connection, or from its resulting loyalties. But I think you're more susceptible to it if you're a child, or, at least, childish. I was both when I made my first real connection—to pro football: the Green Bay Packers, to be precise. Among the great Green Bay players of that halcyon time, each fan had his own gladiator, his private Packer, a gridiron version of Chiyonofuji who transcended the confusion on the TV screen. Mine?

As I recall, he would seize the ball as a mean little kid might snatch candy from his baby brother, and then he'd plunge into a Gordian tangle of bodies. Gone. Finished. But then—somehow—in a churning, clawing, slobbering frenzy, he would burst out on the other side, dragging people, shrugging them off, and then looking up, looking around. For what?

More people to run into! Instead of running for the open field, he would charge into crowds, assault them, knock them down and step on their heads. He was the quintessential fullback: Jim Taylor. If not Taylor, or Paul Hornung the Platonic halfback, or Ray Nitschke, the archetypal linebacker—or even football!—then Ruth, Williams and Koufax in baseball. Willie Mays! Or Tilden in tennis. Bobby Jones in golf. Pele, Bobby Hull, Bill Russell. Some players are so good that you feel it, even if you've never seen the sport before. They seduce you with awe and hold you with compassion. You want them always to be just that great and never grow old. Until you care that way, vicariously and irrationally, about what happens to the players, there's no point in knowing names, discussing technique, or tracing bloodlines.

The nice thing about sumo is that, once you have the connection, you're looking at men in jockstraps— much easier to tell apart than whole teams of guys with helmets, numbers, identical uniforms, and spiked elbow pads. If he's up to it, each sumo combatant gets a solo shot, every day, to simulate the savagery of the fullback, the grace of the halfback, or the surgical violence of the free safety. This exposure helps the fan to learn the wrestlers' bodies, oddities, tendencies, coaches, names—all that useless stuff— surprisingly fast.

Nomenclature: Proper and Improper

But, if you can discover the hero, achieve that connection, what's next?

Well, you cannot hold your head up, as a real fan, if you only recognize one or two favorite studs. You have to learn them all. Names. You need names—what they are, who they are.

First, you have to know what to call them, as a group. If you wanna be a serious, know-it-all fan (and who doesn't?) you should probably stop calling them "sumo wrestlers," which is redundant because "sumo" is "wrestling." The most correct term is probably *rikishi* ("big strong bastard"), but lots of experts prefer *sumotori*—which I like, too, because if you screw up the translation badly enough, it comes out as "street fighter"—which nicely denotes the proletarian ambience of sumo. Sumo nerds will also confuse you with the term *sekitori,* which means, simply, a rikishi in one of the upper two divisions of sumo (makuuchi and juryo, remember?).

Actually, Junko and I sometimes just lapse into calling the guys "sumo" (plural: "sumos"), which is a little like calling Phil Esposito a hockey puck. But heck, if the shoe fits . . .

When it's all in the family, on your own TV, you can call a sumo wrestler anything you want (including "sumo wrestler"). If "lardass" strikes your fancy—as in, "Hey, who's that lardass wrestling Chiyonofuji?"—why not? Especially if you end up cheering for Lardass in his next match. There's something mystical in the act of name-giving, even when you do it in derision. Once you've given this stranger your own private ID tag, you start to care about what happens to him.

This is how I came to know, and love, an old warhorse of the dohyo named Ozutsu. If ever there were an archetypal fat homely rikishi, it's old

Ozutsu—who battles tooth-and-nail with the second-rate wrestlers, but goes down irritably in flames when he faces one of the stars. Ozutsu's dubious distinction is that a large share of the fat in his body migrated to his face, puffing it up like a terminal case of mumps and squeezing his lips into a permanent, pudgy, protuberant "O." He looks like a goldfish in a Warner cartoon, so—irresistibly—we began to call him "The Goldfish."

Once we had saddled Ozutsu with that degrading label, we began to watch his matches more closely—and more affectionately. We began to notice his occasional moments of exceptional cunning, and the passion with which he fought, even in a hopeless mismatch.

I didn't know it at the time, but Ozutsu's chosen name is also evocative. "Ozutsu" translates as "Enormous Cannon," or simply, "The Big Gun." Either the Goldfish himself, or his oyakata (coach) hung this one on him, for good karma, in 1978, after he'd wrestled—without much distinction—for seven years under another name. Change your name and change your luck! This is standard procedure. The naming of rikishi, like T.S. Eliot's naming of cats, is a blend of gravity and comedy, tradition and whimsy. And, like Eliot's cats, everybody has (at least) three names.

Every rikishi enters the lists with his family name, provided by Mom and Dad. Eventually, he consults with his oyakata, perhaps peruses the honor roll of his sumobeya for inspiration from a heroic forebear, perhaps seizes upon some mystic force in the ecology of his home prefecture, to devise his fighting name.

And then, finally, on retirement, for a whole fresh dose of good karma, the rikishi adopts a new name—creating confusion that usually lingers for the rest of his life, because people insist on remembering him by his fighting name. This requires the addition of an obligatory middle name: "Formerly," as in "Futagoyama Formerly Wakanohana," and "Azumazeki Formerly Takamiyama."

Getting back to Ozutsu, he added a fourth name in the midst of the confusion. In '78, he decided that his first fighting name, "Daishin," was sending out bad vibes. So, presto-chango, he was Ozutsu. In August, 1990, for instance, Takanohama (whom we prefer to call "Frankenstein") changed his name to Toyonoumi—probably because people were getting him mixed up with his coach, Fujishima Formerly Takanohana. We suspect this name change was specified by Coach Fujishima/Takanohana himself, because he was embarrassed by a too-close association with Frankenstein—who is not really somebody you want to be mistaken for.

Ideally, this fighting-name business provides the rikishi with a talisman that sends him soaring into the ring surrounded by the winged blessings of a hundred friendly spirits. Many such fighting names, translated, summon forceful imagery. "Hokutoumi" means "Northern Victory Sea." "Owakamatsu" is "Big Young Pine Tree" and "Kirishima" means "Foggy Island."

Others are weird. "Kotoinazuma" (whom we think of as "Baby Huey") comes out as something like "Lightning Guitar." He might be a Chuck Berry fan. And "Itai," if you callously disregard the Japanese characters while translating (which makes Japanese a much funnier language anyway) means "Ouch!"

Still other sumo-fighting names are better left untranslated because they sound, well, sissy. "Hananokuni" means "Land of Flowers."

For gaijin fans, however, and for many Japanese—who need to consult a dictionary to make sense of many sumo names—official rikishi nomenclature tends to be polysyllabic, unpronounceable, and forbidding. Consider, for example, the dilemma posed by Kitakachidoki. This is why the nicknaming impulse, whether you call him "The Goldfish" or "The Big Gun," is so valuable to the new fan. Regardless of the sport, jocks are easier to pronounce, easier to remember, easier to love, even easier to forgive, when they have lyrical labels. Mudcat Grant! Oil Can Boyd! Pigpen Dwyer! Catfish Hunter! The Juice! The Cooz! Dr. J! Dr. K! Earl the Pearl! Wilt the Stilt! Shoeless Joe! Marvelous Marvin! Swift Current Fats! And so on, deliciously.

Endowed with that funny name, a name of your very own invention, the Goldfish, or even "the sweaty one," tends to grow on you. The connection wraps around you like the tentacles of an octopus. When you devise your own nicknames, it is as though you have partaken in the creation of the very human being himself.

Sumo is vulnerable to do-it-yourself embellishment—in the spirit of baseball philosopher J. Henry Waugh and his creator, Robert Coover—because its organizers are so unhelpful to the fan. That's one reason I enjoy it! The Sumo Association doesn't really encourage the public to invent frivolous pet names for rikishi. Japanese sportswriters and sportscasters are careful to toe that line. Diz and PeeWee do not man the mikes in the sumo league. But all the better. For us compulsive hypocorists, the approval of officialdom is an unwelcome intrusion.

Of course, not every jock deserves a nickname. On Steve Garvey or Rick Barry, Gale Sayers or Jay Berwanger, it would have hung unnaturally, like a Day-Glo necktie on a Shiite mullah. But Duke Snider and Moose Skowron would've been naked without their nicknames. With Rogers Hornsby, Joe Paterno, Dave Cowens, Lawrence Taylor, the full Christian name conveys the only proper scansion. But there are others for whom the nickname alone is name enough: Boog, Goose, Whitey, Tiny, Big Daddy, Bad News, Too Tall, Hondo, the Bronx Bomber, the Mad Stork, the Golden Bear . . .

There are more than 60 rikishi in sumo's upper two divisions, and Junko and I have deemed less than 20 (so far) worthy of nicknames. Others will grow nicknames, by and by, but only as fast as they demonstrate a measure of walk, personality, talk, personality, style, personality . . .

Herewith, a sample. Fifteen whom we've come to love, beginning of course, with the sweaty one.

1) The sweaty one is Fujinoshin. The first time we saw him, he was wearing a light blue mawashi (belt) which was stained and soaked with perspiration. He probably could've wrung it out into a bucket and gotten enough fluid to float his bathtub ducky. What else to call him? With apologies to Horshack, Barbarino and Juan Epstein: "The Sweathog!"

2) Ozutsu, for reasons already explained, is "The Goldfish."

3) Akebono, or Chad Rowan, is a young, very tall Hawaiian who has grown—atop his thin legs—a spectacular rotundity, around which he has affixed a brilliant orange mawashi. We call him "The Great Pumpkin."

4) Ryogoku (no, his name just sounds the same as the sumo hall) has one of the weirdest shapes in sumo—an immense, dense torso and very short legs. It might befit him, but no, we don't call him anything nearly so dignified as "Toulouse-Lautrec." Watching other rikishi struggle with Ryogoku is like watching a trash collector trying to lift a plastic garbage can after a heavy rain—bottom-heavy with water and disgustingly unstable. His nickname: "Trashcan."

5) Wakasegawa is round-shouldered, cute in a grumpy sort of way, and he's the only rikishi with hair on his back—suggesting, of course, a teddy bear. We call him "Paddington."

6) Despite a long career of almost unrelieved mediocrity, Enazakura occasionally distinguishes himself with an inspired tournament. During one of these rare fits of competence, we started cheering him on, noticed his bright violet mawashi, and started calling him the "Purple Prince." Sometime in his life, everyone should be blessed with a slightly overwrought nickname. I was once briefly known, f'rinstance, as "The Fastest Man in Hull House Camp." But that's another story.

7) Kotoinazuma is one of our favorites. We call him "Baby Huey" because he's really so small and huggable, his mawashi used to be baby blue and he fights the bigger guys with an irresistible and

unmistakeable look of infantile determination on his face.

8) Kushimaumi is a vast, powerful amoeba. He established his identity with the alert Tokyo sumo audience by raising his arms just before a match, throwing his head back and leaning backward as far as he could reach. It was like a human taffy pull. After noticing this through a tournament or two, the ladies in the Pit started looking forward to this grandiloquent gesture, held their breath in rapt anticipation and then responded—each time—with a sensuous sigh. In tribute, we call him "Stretch."

9) In a short period of time in 1989–90, two brothers entered the juryo class—with enormous publicity—at a very tender age: Takahanada (then 17 years old) and his older brother Wakahanada (18). Herded along by the press-agentry of the Sumo Association, they achieved swift and immense popularity. They deserved it, of course, because they were very young and gifted, and—most important— their father, Takanohana (actually, now he's called Fujishima Oyakata), is a famous former rikishi with his own sumobeya (stable) and lots of status in the Sumo Association. The boys are, indeed, beloved of the gods and programmed for a quick ascent to the pinnacle of sumo. We call them, simply, the "Silver Spoons." Wakahanada is "Big Spoon," Takahanada is "Little Spoon."

10) Tochinowaka is strong, easily distracted, belligerent, and reportedly a pretty nasty guy at home as well. Best of all, he has a face like a Mafia bodyguard. To fit the image, he needed the right nickname: "Big Al." This doesn't make him any more lovable, but at least it wreathes him in a kind of dark glamor.

11) One of the disadvantages to putting on a lot of weight, even in a good cause, is that it can make a young man look a lot like a young woman. The best recent example of this phenomenon was a makuuchi wrestler named Hananoumi, whom we came to know, affectionately, as the "Fat Girl." However, he had to retire because of a very bad back—a common sumo ailment. This left Takamisugi alone among rikishi as the guy most likely to show up as a transsexual's blind date. We call him the "Fat Housewife," or the "Housewife," for short. And he is short.

12) We saw Daishoyama smile once. It was adorable. Now, to us, he's just "Dimples."

13) Mitoizumi is a special case. You either love him or hate him. Another rikishi whose size far exceeds his ability, he performs nevertheless with an almost insufferable insouciance. He wears a garish mawashi, hits himself in the face before every match and, when performing a simple salt-throwing ritual just before the faceoff, turns it into a grand production by throwing the entire contents of the saltbox at the ceiling. He smiles impishly when he wins and limps self-piteously when he loses. He's a ham actor and an adolescent showoff. His nickname is spontaneous, because he is the sort of character you react to, the minute you see him on TV. You say, "Who IS that asshole?" Hence, even though we've come to like him more than we usually admit, we still call Mitoizumi "The Asshole."

14) Tomoefuji, boyish and pudgy, resembles the cover baby on a package of Japan's most popular disposable diapers. So, with no apologies whatsoever

forthcoming to the Unification Church, we call him, "Moonie."

15) Ryukozan, shortly after completing his first makuuchi basho, died at the age of 22, probably of being simply too fat for such a small body. He recalled Maupassant's words, " . . . Short, perfectly spherical, fat as dripping, with puffy fingers, dented at the joints like strings of sausages . . . " Better than any rikishi we've ever seen, Ryukozan had attained that perfect rotund egg-shape that so often depicts sumo wrestlers in cartoons. In honor of that, we named him "Humpty Dumpty," and in his honor, we have retired that nickname devoutly. We will only apply it again to a rikishi who is as willing as was Ryukozan to risk his life for the sake of the perfect bod.

Today, I can impress friends and bore total strangers at parties by rattling off the sanctioned names of virtually every rikishi in the upper two divisions of sumo, and attach the names to a face, a bellybutton, a set of mannerisms, a rank, even a sumobeya—all because, at the beginning, I taught myself these identities through the shorthand of nicknaming. When I place my label on a rikishi, inevitably his chosen name attaches itself and infiltrates my memory.

By the time you read this book, many of the rikishi listed here might have retired or been demoted. But this is good for you, because instead of accepting my dumb nicknames you'll be making up your own according to your own impulses. The key is not the names themselves, but the nicknaming habit, which

BIG AL AND THE SILVER SPOONS • **54**

is as old as sport itself. It tends to concentrate your mind. It helps you to examine each player as a distinct personality and watch him—as he goes through his stalking dance—for the word, the term, the description that is his very essence, his message to mankind . . .

> *His ineffable effable*
> *Effanineffable*
> *Deep and inscrutable singular Name.**

* Eliot, T.S., *Old Possum's Book of Practical Cats*, Harcourt, Brace & World, New York, 1967: p. 12

THE "GROUPING URGE"
Blubberbutts and Thoroughbreds

OK, sports fans, now you're up to the point where you're remembering the jocks, and bandying around pet names as though you suck down prairie oysters with these guys every morning at Kenji's Bar & Grill. The next stage, the inevitable drive, is you're gonna start "studying" them, rikishi by rikishi. It's what fans do.

So, you look close at the TV screen. Now, you've no doubt already dug up an English copy of the Sumo Association's official rankings, or *banzuke,* which can serve as a combination player roster, batting order and racing form. And already, you've noticed the physical differences between these guys, where before you saw only Tweedledum and Tweedledee. As you ponder the subtleties among the bruisers, you feel, swelling in your bosom, a primordial hunger, to break all human beings into groups, species, categories.

This is a natural, wholesome and efficacious instinct. It is also universal. The Japanese have for a long time divided rikishi conveniently into two types, called *ankogata* and *soppugata*. Creatively translated, these come out in English as "blubberbutts" and "thoroughbreds."

Anko are short, fat and relatively unlovely. Soppu are taller, leaner, more athletic and, well, hunkier. These categories are crude, but ingenious in one sense, because they bespeak the most obvious criterion of judgment, the standard that touches us all when we behold sports: the shape of the bod.

The flesh.

Anko and soppu are street words—not profane or obscene, but plain. You will not hear them uttered by NHK's smarmy broadcast team, nor will you often see these two words in the English explanations of sumo, composed by Tokyo's platoon of gaijin sumo experts. Nobody, officially, (if they value the backstage pass issued by the omnipotent Sumo Association) talks about blubberbutts and thoroughbreds.

Which is ridiculous, because it just ain't natural. Talking about guys' looks, comparing, handicapping, categorizing is basic fan intelligence. How else do you decide whom to pull for in a game when you've never seen either team? How else do you choose up sides for kickball at recess on the first day of school? Show me a sumo expert who doesn't harbor a personal preference for either the fat guys or the muscle guys, and I'll show you a phony fan.

Left/Right/Up/Down and All That

However, even NHK flacks and sumo nerds feel the unspoken law of sports that demands some sort of taxonomy, the "grouping urge." Since they eschew the obvious criteria for rikishi comparison, the sanctioned experts resort to more esoteric means. They classify rikishi by means of their favorite grips.

Ask the sumo nerd about, say, Asahifuji, and he'll tell you Asahifuji likes a *migi-yotsu* (right-hand) grip on the other fat guy's belt, while Chiyonofuji, by contrast, was happier with a *hidari-yotsu* (left hand) grip. Often, said nerd will interject additional phrases that indicate whether the rikishi prefers his dominant-hand grip to be under *(shita)* or over *(uwa)* his opponent's corresponding arm.

Nice to know, but it's goddamn hard to follow. These classifications aren't as simple as watching a baseball player settle into the third-base batter's box, thereby prompting the safe assumption that he's a right-handed hitter. Sumo wrestlers don't give you that much time to figure which hand is where.

In a sumo match of, say, five seconds' duration, in which two rikishi are spinning in circles and flailing their arms at each other, determining with the naked eye who got his left arm over the other guy's right arm so he could get his left hand on the right side of the other guy's belt (not to mention which one got his right arm under the other guy's left arm so he could get his right hand on the left side of the other guy's belt) could be just enough of a distraction to ruin the whole five seconds for you. And when it all happens in five seconds anyway, does it really matter where anybody's hands were?

Nevertheless, sumo pedants take pride in pointing out the left/right/up/down orientation of this rikishi or that rikishi, and bleating triumphantly when the two wrestlers demonstrate their tendencies in combat. If you know this stuff, it's fun showing off. I'm a little ashamed, but I even do it myself. And sometimes, this is vital knowledge. If you know, for instance, that Chiyonofuji never—ever—lost when he got a left-hand, inside grip on his opponent's mawashi, you had the key to watching the Champ's matches. Every opponent tried to keep that goddamn left hand away from his belt, and they almost always failed. Chiyonofuji's left hand was in the same league as Sugar Ray Robinson's. But, if the other guy succeeded in fighting off that deadly left, then you had suspense, excitement, magic!—because you knew Chiyo was improvising! To get an idea of how the fan feels when he knows Chiyonofuji is winging it, picture Gene Kelly walking alone in the moonlight with a new tune in his head, or Picasso left by himself in front of a blank white wall, with a grease pencil in his hand.

But that's the exception. Often, a rikishi simply isn't talented enough to execute his favorite grip more than two or three times in a basho. You can watch his every match for two years before figuring out exactly what the hell the poor shnook is trying to do with his hands. Often, two experienced rikishi will block each other's favorite grips, forcing both of them to wrestle from weakness rather than strength. But how does the fan know this? None of this esoteric "grip" classification is easy to spot. You can watch sumo for years without seeing this much fine detail.

And yet, this migi-yotsu/hidari-yotsu, shitate/

uwate business is the approved first-choice Method, among sumo insiders, for grouping the fat guys. Obviously, when you talk about their hands, rather than their tummies, you lend to sumo wrestlers (and their overseers in the Sumo Association) a welcome note of dignity. But the obfuscation and euphemizing that seems to clutter the business of telling the fat ones apart from the sleek ones isn't simply a matter of false dignity.

The strongest reason, I think, for this left-right/up-down riddle, is religious. Sumo's curators, on the Japanese side, are a quasi-priesthood of officious reactionaries, and on the gaijin side, an apple-polishing society of culturemongers. Ideally, these guardians present rikishi to the public not as individuals with great big whopping differences in shape, style and personality, but as mute acolytes of national orthodoxy. In this distorted lens, the differences among the rikishi are subtleties of wrist and leverage. The players are, otherwise, homogeneous, a unified group whose victories and defeats are insignificant. Their importance, in the Shintoist/culturist scheme, is that they preserve a ritual pastime that bespeaks the beauty and impenetrability of things Japanese.

This is not just unrealistic. It's harmful to the sport. Most of the problems of sumo spring directly from this cloistered viewpoint. Fortunately, at least two factors confound the elders' efforts to mummify sumo. First, the rikishi themselves are too distinctive and vital to all sing alto in the plainsong chorus. They are competitors. Their matches are not rehearsed sets of responses and genuflections on a sandy altar. The rikishi go out there hungry, crafty and wired.

They wanna win. They grab, jab, gouge, claw and smack each other in the chops. They do stuff that athletes—real athletes—are supposed to do, can't help but do. They're not dignified, but they're fun.

The crowd comes because the wrestlers are sincere and the game is fun—and this is the other factor that undermines sumo's religionists. The fans feel the tension and share the drama. They study the jocks, learn their gestures and idiosyncracies, divide them up according to bodies, emotions, strength, age, speed, hometowns and home stables, cuteness and ugliness, bellybuttons, even righthandedness and lefthandedness.

Which gets us back, finally, to sumo's great standoff—ankogata or soppugata, to feed or not to feed? There is not a barroom sumo discussion anywhere in Japan that doesn't eventually get around to this timeless, passionate quandary. Muscle or fat. Beauty or blubber. This is Japan's version of Ruth-or-Maris, Chamberlain-or-Russell, Coe-or-Ovett, DH-or-no DH.

Begin it a thousand times and it will ignite discussion at the same point and spin it in the same circle. It will engage, with equal claim to authority, the expert and the amateur, the novice and the oldtimer, the know-it-all and the pupil, the once-in-a-whiler and the junkie. The "grouping urge," always based on the idea that there are two kinds of people, is the raw material of the fan, the wisdom of the playground, the DNA of sports fans group jocks instinctively because, heck, it's fun. But classifying jocks draws you, connects you more and more deeply, because it teaches you so much! Based on the guy's looks, you can make remarkably accurate assumptions about what to expect from a particular jock. Line up all the guards in the National Basketball Association, for instance. The well-schooled hoop fan, even if he prefers college ball and doesn't know any of the NBA guys by name or reputation, can—with an impressive degree of accuracy, simply by comparing their bodies—divide them into the various categories that apply to their position. You have, for instance, point guards, shooting guards, swingmen and defensive specialists, plus your big-guard and your small-guard types, guards who penetrate and guards who pull up. And then, there's the occasional pure genius (Magic Johnson).

And of course—this is the best part—you can be totally fooled. Muggsy Bogues and Charles Barkley certainly don't look like basketball players. Maradona doesn't look like a world-class soccer player, and Johnny Unitas never looked like a football star.

Genus and Species

All of which boils down to the inescapable conclusion that ankogata and soppugata are, on the one hand, invaluable terms in the appreciation of the sport of sumo, and, on the other hand, simply not enough. Breaking the rikishi down to only two categories is wonderful and addictive, but it's sloppy. A guy like Takanofuji, f'rinstance, is neither fat nor lissom, soft nor hard, big nor small, and he's almost supernaturally mediocre. He doesn't fit either slot.

I attacked this basic challenge of rikishi taxonomy early in my own sumo education, long before I knew the words ankogata and soppugata existed. I began with as many as 12 different classifications, realized

I'd gotten carried away, and then reduced that number to eight. My second cut got me down to five, but it was not a well-sifted five.

So I thought again. Finally, I recognized that properly, beneath the Genus Anko (Blubberbutt), there are two distinct species of rikishi, your Hippos and your Butterballs. Beneath the Genus Soppu (Thoroughbred), two species also stand forth, your Jocks and your Cabdrivers.

A foolish consistency, however—as Emerson nagged—is the hobgoblin of little minds. As I organized my rikishi according to my own typology, I noticed some mixing of genus and species (as you will see in the list on pp. 69–70). It is rare but possible for an ankogata kind of guy, like Akinoshima, to be a Jock. Wesley Unseld, after all, was a pretty nimble endomorph! And there are frequent examples— Tochitsukasa, f'rinstance—of the ankogata Cabdriver. But more on this later.

In a little more detail, here is the definitive Benjamin Taxonomy of rikishi and how you can tell them apart.

1) JOCKS. A Jock is someone who'd be an athlete even if sumo didn't exist. Jocks, despite a perpetual size disadvantage, have always dominated sumo's highest two ranks, yokozuna and ozeki. Chiyonofuji, for example, who might be the most athletic rikishi of this century, ranked—in 1990—25th in height among 38 makuuchi division wrestlers, and 35th in weight.

With Chiyonofuji as their model, Jocks defy the perception that all sumo wrestlers are fat boys who flunked the junior high entrance exam and got shipped off to the local sadist by their despairing dads. Jocks, in a nutshell, are compact, muscular, usually quick and shockingly agile for their size. Some of them (including Chiyonofuji) have defied the advice of their coaches and built up their strength through rigorous weight training programs—using, in the process, "Western" technology, like Nautilus machines.

It's conventional to assert that, as a rule, Jocks tend to be technically more sophisticated than rikishi in the other three species, because they must compensate for their weight disadvantage. However, there are actually many Jocks whose wrestling skills are suspect and who tend to rely on a blend of sheer athleticism and brute force. Chiyonofuji's stablemate Hokutoumi—the Jake LaMotta of sumo—is foremost in this category.

2) HIPPOS. The secret of being a Hippo is in your glands. If you're a little taller than the average bear and possess an almost infinite capacity for gaining weight without collapsing from a series of stress fractures all over your grotesque body—and you can still move—you are a rare and unnatural deposit. And you're scary as hell ("Oh my God, Helen! It's moving!"), 'cause hardly anybody knows what to do with them. Konishiki (real name, Salévaa Atisanoe), a Samoan/Hawaiian behemoth who once weighed in at 253 kg (557 pounds), is the ultimate Hippo. In recent times, his only challenger for the title of Weight Watchers' Public Enemy Number One was yokozuna Onokuni, who hit 211 kg (462 pounds) before gravity and cholesterol began wreaking revenge on his health. The most promising Hippo-in-

waiting, as this book is being written, is Kushimaumi ("Stretch"), a mere sylph at 185kg (407 pounds), but growin' fast.

Nobody would ever beat Hippos if they could get out of their own way. The TV commentators regularly gush about Hippos being "quick" for their size—a questionable assertion when you realize that no one has really put together a sample group of 500-pound people to find out how quick they are, not to mention the problem of convincing them to all run the 40-yard dash, so you can draw up a bell curve. An NHK color man praising a Hippo for his quickness is the equivalent of his NBC counterpart saying that pitcher Al Nipper is "sneaky fast." It's an excuse, not an insight. With Hippos, quickness is the issue, because it's what they ain't got. Konishiki, for instance, in terms of sheer mass, is four people, and he's only got two legs. Try getting four people with eight legs to move together in a hurry and you have a sense of your average Hippo's mobility. There are escalators that are shiftier.

As Onokuni (who retired in 1991 at age 28) demonstrated also, the burden of bulk tends to erode Hippos' competitive intensity and shorten their careers. Being a Hippo is like being John Wayne's horse—except the son of a bitch never gets off your back. Asashio, for example, a delightful character who qualified as a pygmy Hippo, retired late in 1989 at age 32, after several wretched tournaments. By contrast, Kirishima the Jock won promotion in 1990—at age 31—to ozeki, sumo's second highest rank; and Chiyonofuji was still winning basho in 1991 at age 34. Hippos blossom early and decline young. Jocks are late bloomers.

3) BUTTERBALLS. These are the guys the inexperienced fan thinks of when he pictures sumo. Butterballs are short, fat and mediocre—which is one reason why some people call them Rotarians. The funny thing about Butterballs is you tend to love one on sight or hate 'im—because he either looks like a teddy bear (current examples: Kotogaume, Itai) or a pig (Daishoyama, Ozutsu). Of course, one man's Pooh is another man's Porky. I've developed a grudging admiration for the really ugly Butterballs, like the Goldfish, and I tend to detest the cute ones.

The Goldfish typifies one of the insidious charms of Butterballs. More than Jocks, Butterballs step onto the dohyo every day with a chronic disadvantage. Although they have succeeded in the cherished sumo aspiration of dumpling themselves into dangerous obesity, they haven't been able to match this inflation with an expansion of their natural talent. Survival, for the average Butterball, depends on his wits, on his knowledge of his opponents, his application of a few favorite moves and the wisdom never to wrestle beyond his abundant limitations. The Butterball, with self-preservation as his prime directive, has long since replaced, in his outlook, the pride of the tiger with the sneakiness of the shithouse rat.

Because they're so round, stumpy, homely and average, it takes time for Butterballs to grow on you. But Butterball love really does blossom. It starts with pity and moves up to sympathy, and then—though you might not feel it happening—you start to identify. You look in the mirror, notice your own spare tire, the old pimple scars, the bags under your eyes, the five o'clock shadow at 11 a.m. You think about all the daily defeats and indignities that grind you into the

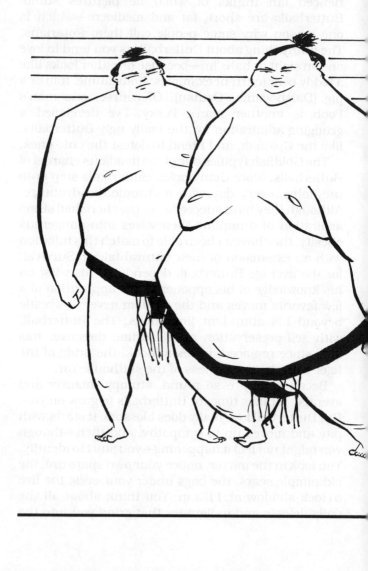

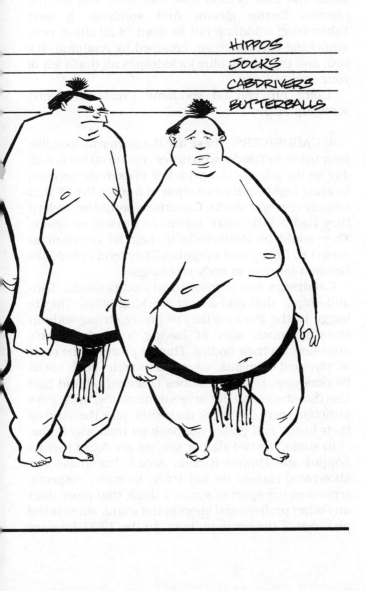

sand. You look behind that dull stare and see the coyote's furtive gleam. And suddenly it isn't Takamisugi waddling out in front of all those rice-munching voyeurs to get creamed by Asahifuji. It's you, and that shiny blue jockstrap is all that's left of your ego.

"Come on, you fat goddamn Housewife! Don't screw up again!"

4) CABDRIVERS. These are the guys who look like your uncle in Toledo, who never gets up off his ass all day on the job, doesn't get a lick of exercise between bowling nights and has a chair in front of the TV that nobody else ever sits in. Cabdrivers would be Jocks if they had a little more talent, or muscle or desire. They could be Butterballs if their fat distribution wasn't so lumpy and irregular. They tend to look like German tourists in body stockings.

Cabdrivers are sumo's meat-and-potatoes, fish-and-chips, shot-and-a-beer working stiffs. They're baggy in the gut and they're pretty strong without showing much sign of having a whole muscle anywhere on their bodies. They're prone to the sorts of physical ailments we all live with: sore backs (Wakasegawa), kidney stones (Takanofuji) and hair loss (Sasshunada). But aches or no aches, these guys punch in every day, work their shift, pick the sand off their butts, and grab a six-pack on their way home.

In sumo, the two glamor species are Jocks (Genus Soppu) and Hippos (Genus Anko). But these two showpiece classes do not truly, in many respects, represent the sport of sumo. I think that more than any other professional sport in the world, sumo is the province of the common man. In the 1990 January

Basho, for example, 30 of the top 50 rikishi were cannon fodder: Butterballs and Cabdrivers.

According to the Benjamin Taxonomy, which is, of course, subjective and largely arbitrary, here is the breakdown of genus and species among the top 50 rikishi in that highly typical tournament.

Name	Official Rank	Genus	Species
MAKUUCHI DIVISION			
1. Chiyonofuji	Yokozuna	Soppu	Jock
2. Hokutoumi	Yokozuna	Soppu	Jock
3. Onokuni	Yokozuna	Anko	Hippo
4. Konishiki	Ozeki	Anko	Hippo
5. Asahifuji	Ozeki	Soppu	Jock
6. Hokutenyu	Ozeki	Soppu	Jock
7. Mitoizumi	Sekiwake	Anko	Hippo
8. Kotogaume	Sekiwake	Anko	Butterball
9. Terao	Sekiwake	Soppu	Jock
10. Kirishima	Komusubi	Soppu	Jock
11. Ryogoku	Komusubi	Anko	Hippo
12. Kasugafuji	Maegashira #1	Anko	Butterball
13. Ozutsu	Maegashira #1	Anko	Butterball
14. Tochitsukasa	Maegashira #2	Anko	Cabdriver
15. Sakahoko	Maegashira #2	Soppu	Cabdriver
16. Itai	Maegashira #3	Anko	Butterball
17. Kotoinazuma	Maegashira #3	Soppu	Cabdriver
18. Tochinowaka	Maegashira #4	Soppu	Cabdriver
19. Wakasegawa	Maegashira #4	Anko	Cabdriver
20. Takanofuji	Maegashira #5	Soppu	Cabdriver
21. Enazakura	Maegashira #5	Soppu	Cabdriver
22. Kotonishiki	Maegashira #6	Soppu	Jock
23. Akinoshima	Maegashira #6	Anko	Jock
24. Hananokuni	Maegashira #7	Soppu	Cabdriver
25. Daijuyama	Maegashira #7	Anko	Butterball
26. Kyokudozan	Maegashira #8	Soppu	Jock
27. Kotofuji	Maegashira #8	Soppu	Cabdriver
28. Kushimaumi	Maegashira #9	Anko	Hippo

Name	Official Rank	Genus	Species
MAKUUCHI DIVISION *(cont'd)*			
29. Jingaku	Maegashira #9	Soppu	Cabdriver
30. Misugisato	Maegashira #10	Soppu	Cabdriver
31. Ryukozan	Maegashira #10	Anko	Butterball
32. Takanohama	Maegashira #11	Anko	Hippo
33. Oginohana	Maegashira #11	Soppu	Jock
34. Tagaryu	Maegashira #12	Anko	Butterball
35. Takamisugi	Maegashira #12	Anko	Butterball
36. Kirinishiki	Maegashira #13	Anko	Butterball
37. Kinoarashi	Maegashira #13	Anko	Butterball
38. Koboyama	Maegashira #14	Anko	Butterball
JURYO DIVISION			
39. Asahisato	Juryo #1	Soppu	Cabdriver
40. Kitakachidoki	Juryo #1	Soppu	Cabdriver
41. Saganobori	Juryo #2	Soppu	Jock
42. Sasshunada	Juryo #2	Anko	Butterball
43. Owakamatsu	Juryo #3	Soppu	Cabdriver
44. Hananofuji	Juryo #3	Soppu	Cabdriver
45. Dairyu	Juryo #4	Anko	Butterball
46. Kyokugozan	Juryo #4	Anko	Butterball
47. Kototsubaki	Juryo #5	Soppu	Cabdriver
48. Hoshiiwato	Juryo #5	Anko	Butterball
49. Isshinriki	Juryo #6	Soppu	Jock
50. Takahanada	Juryo #6	Soppu	Jock

Don't let all this orderliness fool you. I could be wrong.

If you've watched a half dozen basho, you probably think about ten of these classifications are outright stupid. For instance, what the heck am I doing classifying a couple of pachyderms like Kotogaume and Kyokugozan as Butterballs?

Well, I reply patiently, the measure of a Hippo is not just mass but height. Kotogaume and Kyokugozan are short guys, and moreover, they have that broad, cuddly roundness that bespeaks the very concept of "Butterball."

Bullshit!—you retort. Well, everyone to his own opinion. If I were you, frankly, I'd dispute the classification of Tochinowaka (Big Al)—compact, quick, muscular, and dangerous—as a Cabdriver. He has all the physical characteristics of a Jock.

So, why not call him a Jock? I'll tell you why not, Mawashi-breath! Because Big Al doesn't have the heart of a Jock! He gives his full effort only once in three basho, he refuses to study his sport and his opponents with the intensity of a superior athlete, and he wastes his potential. Looks like a Jock, fights like a hack.

Players like Kotogaume and Tochinowaka are the types often spoken of in other sports as "tweeners," athletes whose individual traits overlap the categories created by professional scouts and disseminated by sportswriters. Former Notre Dame basketball coach Digger Phelps might have been the most successful trainer of tweeners in modern sports. His program produced a series of outstanding unclassifiables whose talent and determination often transcended the oddity of their shape: Bill Hanzlik, Bill Laimbeer, Kelly Tripucka, Adrian Dantley.

In short, the Benjamin Taxonomy is not authoritative. It definitely lacks logic. And it's not very respectful.

So what? If you don't agree with it, go ahead. When the next basho comes along, make your own list. Or make up your own categories. If you prefer three groups, or five, or 10, go ahead—that's the spirit!

Categories, in fact, are pointless without disagreements (which is why the Sumo Association's ex cathedra rankings are so dull). The arguments, actually, are the life of the party. The quality that distinguishes the real fan from the dilettante is that he argues at the drop of a hat, or a name, or a stat— instantly, tirelessly and obnoxiously. He argues about points that can never be settled, about statistics that don't exist, about events that never happened, about imaginary teams.

The "grouping urge" is one of the fountainheads of such sports arguments. More people in, say, Milwaukee, in one day, spend more words and energy inventing, revising and disputing sports categories— often in homicidal language—than the rest of the people in the world burn up on discussions of population control or deficit spending.

(Listen, I've checked on this. It's true.)

So, if by doubling the available number of rikishi categories, I have added even 10 percent to the volume of argument about sumo, well, that's terrific, because it means I've made the sport more contentious—and therefore more fun for regular people.

You know. The guys down at Kenji's Bar & Grill.

BACKSTAGE

Choking Up in the Church

Most sports reporting is incompetent. I'm entitled to say this, because I've done my own share of nitwit sportswriting.

However, though sportwriters are the smegma of journalism, the fatuity of their output isn't entirely their fault, because sports readers tend toward ignorant expectations. In sports with scores, your average Associated Press postgame roundup begins with the final score and ends by describing a decisive hit or shot or goal that led thereto, or maybe the grand total of Butch Dewlapp, high scorer. In a race, the story inevitably dwells on the last lap, the final 20 meters, the home stretch or the kick to the tape. In boxing, your conventional sportswriter goes straight to the last round, the telling blows, the final knockdown, and—if there's a little space left over for literary flourish—the puddle of blood on the canvas.

Bylined sportswriters have more freedom, of course, which usually means that they avoid telling you the final score at all, leaving such mundane chores up to the lackey who writes the headlines. It also means that the writer tends to gloss entirely over anything that actually happened in the game, so that he (or she) can proceed directly to an exegesis of the game's "meaning" in the vast scheme of human fates that hang upon the success or failure of the franchise. In either case, you learn very little of what actually happened and, in the worst case, you learn far too much about a witness who—at least according his testimony—was there.

In sumo, this cycle of insipid reportage—especially in English—is narrower, making it all the more oppressive, and abysmally bereft of information. Usually, the post-match analysis is finished when your ringside reporter gives the benediction, which comes in the form of a sesquipedalian phrase signifying the technique that finished off the loser. This polysyllable succinctly defines the relative positions of the two rikishi at the moment the match ended. It is literally the last word on the battle, and it is dispensed with reverence by the commentators.

All sports fans relish this moment of climax, the ephemeral crossing of the border between struggle and decision, but the hardcore sportso—the real fan—wants more. Gimme the score, tell me the grip, but then I wanna know: What was the "turning point"? When did the Big Mo shift? When did the winner smell blood? When did the loser flinch? These are questions that inspire the disputation of sports, that transform spectator into scientist. Such issues transcend the mere brute clash of athletic competition and place it among more exalted intellectual pursuits, geopolitics, military strategy, philosophy, and law.

Napoleon and Konishiki

For instance, your typical sportswriter, covering, say, the Battle of Waterloo, would have hung the whole story on Blucher's dramatic arrival from "the heights round Frischemont" to rescue Wellington and send Napoleon's army into rout. Even Victor Hugo, momentarily, called this "the turning-point." But then, he went on to place much more emphasis on an earlier shift in fate, when Napoleon's magnificent 3,500 mounted cuirassiers, under Milhaud, charged the plateau of Mont-Saint-Jean. As he gave the order [Hugo recalled], Napoleon "ordered a dispatch-rider to ride posthaste to Paris with the news that the battle was won."

Talk about chutzpah, huh? Picture Joe Gibbs ordering the fat lady to sing at halftime of the '89 Super Bowl!

But Gibbs had a flat field and a hot quarterback. Milhaud was a horse of another temperature. Neither Milhaud, nor Ney, Kellermann, Delord, Wathier nor Lefebvre-Desnouette had troubled to scout the battlefield properly and to see that huge crevasse on the approach to Mont-Saint-Jean, the sunken country lane that ran between Braine-l'Alleud and Ohain—where one-third of the attacking cavalry plunged to their deaths.

"It was the beginning of the defeat," said Hugo

during the days of Napoleon. These are the words of a man who studies the game and reads the agate—the words of a real fan.

Most New York fans, reviewing a fairly recent event, the Knicks' extraordinary comeback victory in the first round of the 1990 playoffs, would dwell on the moment in the final period of the fifth game, when the Celtics' Larry Bird clanged a dunk shot and triggered the Knicks' decisive 10–2 scoring run. But a real fan would go back further in time.

To an earlier point in the game? No, long before that—to June, 1986, when Len Bias, the Celtics' first franchise-quality draft pick in six years, assassinated himself with an overdose of coke. That moment turned the Celtics into an aging dynasty with no consistent answer to any opponent with good team speed and an active defense.

Obviously, turning points can occur days before the Big Game, or months or years—often unseen or unheard of by the hapless fan who believes the pap dished out by journeyman sportwriters. This is especially true of sumo, whose action is so shockingly brief that, indeed, the decisions and errors of strategy must always emerge in the prelude to the match.

Consider, for example, the most important match of the 1990 Natsu (Summer, i.e., May) Basho, between Chiyonofuji and Konishiki. For both rikishi, a great deal was at stake—but more so for Chiyonofuji. The great yokozuna was battling against time and posterity. He was close to his 35th birthday, and the speculation that he would soon retire was growing ever louder. Takamiyama, Konishiki's oyakata (head coach) had declared before the basho that

Chiyo was over the hill. Chiyonofuji was already the winner of 30 basho and in the previous one he'd become the first rikishi in history to win 1,000 matches. But in the stubborn memory of the sumo world, Chiyonofuji would remain an ever-so-slightly soiled immortal if he failed to match Taiho's all-time record of 32 tournament championships.

The Natsu Basho title was within Chiyonofuji's grasp as he prepared for his Day 14 match against Konishiki. He was 12–1, tied for the lead with Asahifuji. Of course, Konishiki was a hell of a hurdle to clear. Konishiki outweighed Chiyo 233 kg to 122 kg.

Never mind. Konishiki could be had.

Shinko, a former sekitori who has wrestled both Chiyonofuji and Konishiki and who still stays in the game vicariously through his sumo-motif chankonabe restaurant in Komagome, explained the relationship between Chiyonofuji the master and Konishiki, the young, emotional giant. "Put Chiyonofuji against Konishiki ten times in practice, every day, and every day Chiyonofuji will win nine times. If they wrestled on the first day of every basho, Konishiki would never win. Never."

Coming into Day 14 of the Natsu Basho, Chiyonofuji had not shown his age. He looked really *genki*, a strange word that means "healthy" in Japanese but in Sumospeak means more—confident, well-focused, finely-tuned and lucky.

Until Day 11, Konishiki had kept pace with the leaders. Then, consecutive losses to Stretch and Asahifuji had killed his chances for a *yusho* (tournament win). If Konishiki had managed this yusho, it would have put him squarely in line for promotion to yokozuna, a rank to which no gaijin has ever ascended. The three defeats postponed that goal, but he still needed a good basho record to merit a shot at yokozuna the next time out in July. Nevertheless, though he needed to keep winning, Konishiki faced less pressure than Chiyo.

Also to Konishiki's advantage, he had recently begun to reverse Chiyonofuji's longstanding dominance. Chiyo's overall record against Konishiki was 18-8, but Konishiki had beaten Chiyo three straight. The first in that streak was in the November 1989 Kyushu Basho, when a terrified Konishiki had shocked Chiyonofuji on Day 11, en route to the first yusho of his career. Chiyonofuji won the next basho but lost his match with Konishiki, and Konishiki beat him again in the March basho.

When they finally faced off and charged on Day 14 of the 1990 Natsu Basho, the pattern seemed unaltered. The slap of flesh, a moment of tension and then Konishiki bulled Chiyonofuji off the dohyo. But this time, there was a difference. The turning point was already in the past.

This match was over a long time before it started. Let's go back.

In the Kyushu Basho, six months before, the rhythm and electricity of a great athletic battle hung over the dohyo and intensified as Konishiki and Chiyonofuji met. Konishiki struggled mightily, against an old pro and his own fear. To watch him—to watch both rikishi—was moving and memorable. The turning point came in the first seconds of the fight, when Chiyonofuji's deadly left hand darted toward Konishiki's belt—once, twice, three times. And again! Each time, with great windmill swings of his right arm, Konishiki batted away Chiyonofuji's left.

Konishiki sacrificed his own devastating charge and he fought one-handed. He gave up most of his offense to defend himself against the certain defeat in Chiyonofuji's left. Only when Konishiki had parried Chiyonofuji's fourth thrust could he move in, turn the match in his favor and ride Chiyonofuji off the dohyo.

All right, now jump forward again. Six months later in the Natsu Basho, the hoped-for drama of Chiyonofuji/Konishiki was non-existent. Konishiki's first charge backed Chiyonofuji immediately to the brink. Chiyonofuji bounced several times at Konishiki, kept his left arm curled ineffectually against his chest and made only one sluggish thrust with his right hand. The match was a turkey. Chiyonofuji backpedaled, lost and sat down. Konishiki had had a tougher match four days before against Oginohana, a rookie in his third makuuchi tournament who finished the basho with a 4–11 record.

So what happened?

The word that explains that disappointment is one that every American sports fan knows—which means that, among all the people in the Ryogoku Kokugikan that day, Konishiki is one of the very few who would have understood its application to Chiyonofuji's piss-poor performance. It is perhaps the darkest, most damning word in sports. Spoken aloud to an opponent, it is the gauntlet that guarantees a fight. Addressed to a game official after a disputed call, it means automatic expulsion.

What happened to Chiyonofuji? That's simple.

He choked.

Chiyonofuji was a rikishi who survived with his body but won with his mind. A choke is the offspring of a flaccid mind, a sign that fear has conquered the human will. At some time, it happens to every athlete—to every human being, for that matter. In sports, it is always on naked display, and it's always dangerous to point it out.

That day, in Chiyonofuji's defeat, the choke was on. The choke was the turning point, and it came before the match began. In fact, that match probably turned six months before in Kyushu, when Chiyonofuji discovered that Konishiki could take Chiyo's very best, and whip him.

When I explained the choke to my wife, Junko, she tried to render it as *nigate ishiki*—which can be translated as a "premonition of defeat," or "I got a bad feeling about that son of a bitch," or simply a "tough matchup." Nigate ishiki is a term that applies, for instance, when the Phoenix Suns visit the Forum in L.A., which was (at least until the '90 playoffs) their own Death Valley. Nate Thurmond always gave Wilt Chamberlain fits: nigate ishiki. Roger Clemens can't beat Dave Stewart; Frank Viola, against San Diego, is a rag-arm; and Alex Karras always ate Willie Davis' lunch. Nigate ishiki.

But that's not choking. These classic confrontations might be jinxed. They might be discouraging matchups, but in none of them has there even been a hint of preemptive surrender. On the contrary, Clemens probably works harder against Stewart than against any other opponent in the American League. Asahifuji, in sumo, always has trouble with Akinoshima—which is why, in the Natsu Basho, when he won the title, he attacked Akinoshima all the more aggressively and beat him all the more decisively. Nigate ishiki is the nameless dread that simultaneously spawns self-doubt and inspires stern determination, redoubling both with every disappointment.

The choke is different. It is the public display of self-doubt. It means that you don't, in your gut, believe you belong on the same mat with the other guy. You're not ready. You've thought, and worried and talked yourself out of the game.

In sumo, the choke, and all its lesser psychological variations, play a profound role—very likely more than in any other sport. More goes on before the game, in sumo, than in most other sports, and sumo is far less forgiving to the athlete whose head isn't in the game from the word "go."

In the closest relative to sumo, amateur wrestling, the shortest match I ever saw was 12 seconds long. That's just about twice the average duration of a sumo match. Most wrestling matches last their full six or nine minutes—long enough for a good wrestler to recover from a private funk or a slow start. Adrenaline can save most athletes from choking at the start. Sumo provides no such indulgence. If you're not all there at the split second the other guy jumps into your face, you are history.

The psychological burden of sumo is also greater because of the Sumo Association's diabolical scheduling system. There is no other sport in which the competitor has more than 24 hours—every day for 15 days—to anticipate a match that will last, in most cases, less than ten seconds. The imbalance between anticipation and action is tortuous.

The Locker Room

Shinko, who retired in 1985, was a middling

rikishi. He was the underdog much of the time, so he learned better than most those feelings of anxiety and inferiority—nigate ishiki—that undermine the athlete and incubate the choke.

In each basho, Shinko explained, before the day's matches, the rikishi report to the arena several hours early. In the first half of their preparations, wrestlers talk, especially to the apprentice wrestlers from their own stables who serve as their grooms. These willing lackeys praise the sekitori, strategize with them about the day's match, rub their backs, bring their tea and help dress them for the ring-entering ceremony. Just about every rikishi's routine varies. But almost everyone, in the midst of the daily buildup, pauses to ponder the schedule—for tomorrow.

Tomorrow's schedule. Before every match, each rikishi has two opponents on his mind. Just as he's about to step onto the dohyo against today's opponent—about whom he has been thinking for 24 hours—the Sumo Association posts the name of the opponent he will have to wrestle 24 hours hence.

"As soon as you read the schedule, the younger wrestlers start talking about how to win the next day's match," said Shinko. "Sometimes you say to yourself, 'Oh, I can't beat him. There's no way.' But that can work in your favor, to keep from getting too tense."

Another former rikishi, Kohji Kitao, who competed as Futahaguro, said, "Everything starts from when you know who you'll be wrestling in your next match. Immediately, you start thinking about the weak points of tomorrow's opponent."

Yes, said Kitao Formerly Futahaguro, you can't

help but tear your attention away from now and focus on tomorrow.

"You have to think, remember all the different patterns that all the rikishi have," he said. "It's like a puzzle—and the puzzle is toughest when your next match is one of the younger wrestlers, a new guy. You don't know what their tendencies are, and they can ambush you."

The next morning, after brooding all night over this shifting puzzle and before a new puzzle is revealed by the scheduling fiends, each rikishi plunges into a last-minute practice session. "You have time to prepare," said Kitao/Futahaguro. "You use the young guys, who impersonate your opponent for that day. You do it again and again, until you've found the grip you think will work, and your body memorizes the movements you've practiced. From then until you're in the locker room, your mind keeps returning to the other guy's weaknesses . . . "

For each athlete, in essence, every basho is an unbroken spiral of solitary mind games. But, regardless of the games—or more accurately, because of them—said Shinko, the tension grows, without relief, for 15 days.

"The sitting, the waiting," added Kitao/Futahaguro, speaking of the basho. "That's when you build up this huge load of tension."

And because of the timing of the schedule announcement, the pressure and distraction are always worst in the locker room just before the match. In the last minutes before wrestling against, say, Tochinowaka, a rikishi suddenly finds himself contemplating the tendencies of someone entirely different, like Sakahoko—whom he won't face until tomorrow. Every fan knows that "looking ahead" like this can screw up a jock's concentration even if he isn't prone to choke.

For instance, back to the Natsu Basho, 1990. Kirishima was riding incredibly high. He was on a roll that went back 16 months—when he began a relentless comeback from a 1–14 record in the first basho of 1989. In eight subsequent basho, Kirishima's record was 76–49, with seven victories over yokozuna. He had accomplished the extraordinary feat of improving in eight straight tournaments. He had been promoted to ozeki after 91 basho in the lower ranks (the longest overture in sumo history) and he was 8–0 going into Day 9. For the second consecutive basho, he was in the race for the title.

Kirishima's eighth win the day before had clinched *kachikoshi*, the second most coveted objective—after the yusho—in sumo. Kachikoshi is the magic "8," a majority of victories in the 15-day ordeal; it insures the wrestler against demotion to a lower rank. There are few de-motivators in sport as potent as kachikoshi. And Kirishima had it.

This wasn't just wasn't your everyday garden-variety kachikoshi, either. Kirishima had needed it—and needed it decisively—in his first basho as ozeki, to prove that his 16-month ascent was no fluke. It was vindication for himself and for his oyakata (head coach), Izutsu. Kirishima's kachikoshi-clinching victory the day before was also, dangerously, his first real chance, in more than a year, to lie back and contemplate his success. He was at the top of his game, the toast of Tokyo, and he had an easy match—against Oginohana, an overmatched rookie who had eked out only two victories in eight days. A pushover.

As he prepared for his victory over Oginohana, Kirishima received the Day 10 schedule. He was slated against ozeki Asahifuji—who was always tough, but especially tough in this basho. Irresistibly, Kirishima looked ahead, and blew the yusho.

On the dohyo that day, Kirishima's gait was subtly different. His eyes wandered. He hesitated at *tachiai* (the faceoff). And then he got creamed. While Kirishima was looking forward to Asahifuji, the rookie kicked his ass. And of course, the next day, dwelling on that careless defeat, Kirishima was easy pickings for Asahifuji. After his 8–0 start, Kirishima went 1–6. He didn't choke, but almost as bad—he cracked.

The psychological pressure of sumo has few comparisons. Perhaps the closest parallel was the pre-1991 Super Bowl, which required the players to slog through two weeks of anticipation, preparation, and hype before they finally got to play the game. That's a ratio of 336 hours of anxiety to one hour of football. In sumo, through 15 days of competition, the ratio of anxiety to actual wrestling is 360 hours to 90 seconds.

Because of this unparalleled imbalance between sitting around and throwing punches, the mental fortitude required in sumo is misunderstood by most fans. Chiyonofuji was a brilliant rikishi because his powers of concentration were extraordinary. It is a measure of the pressure that sumo exerts on the human mind that even Chiyonofuji, said to be the iceman of sumo, could psych himself out of a match as totally as he did in that Natsu Basho defeat to Konishiki.

Aprons and Ads

In the midst of the pre-match tension, the rikishi do, however, get a break. They all get dressed up in their aprons and . . .

Aprons? Guys in aprons? Like Dagwood Bumstead doing the dishes?

Well, there's reason for this.

Advertising.

Each apron, or "sumo skirt," is different. The pretty picture on the front is unique, and embroidered just above the fringe is the name of a sponsor who paid for it. "East Hokkaido Sumo Boosters," "Shimonoseki Rotary Club," "Chiba Tool & Die"— that sort of thing. Kind of like the outfield fences in the Carolina League. The rikishi don't have much say in the design of their own sumo skirts, since they're not paying for them. The skirts themselves are slightly more tasteful than a display of oil paintings on black velvet in a K-Mart parking lot, but not as artistically sublime as your average mural of Mt. Fuji in a Tokyo public bath. If your husband, for instance, brought home an only-slightly-soiled sumo skirt, bragging about how he got it cheap and it was actually worn by Asashio in his next-to-last basho, and he started insisting that it should be hung in a prominent place, you'd have to humor him—for the sake of the family's reputation. "It's really beautiful, dear, and I'd love it right above the davenport, but that wouldn't be fair to you."

"Huh? Why not?"

"Well, sweetheart, you're hardly ever in the living room. It would be much better to hang it in the garage—right over your workbench. To inspire you as you . . . create."

"O-oh. Yeah."

Sumo skirts—some of which are sillier than others (Jingaku wears a badly embroidered version of Jonathan Livingston Seagull, Sakahoko lumbers onto the dohyo with an entire iris garden bursting from his loins, and Kyokugozan disports himself with a drowning Brontosaurus)—have never been, as far as I know, criticized on the basis of "artistic impression," for three reasons: 1) Nobody ever criticizes anything in Japan, 2) someone's mom worked her fingers to the bone sewing that incredible thing, and 3) sumo wrestlers have always worn sumo skirts. It's traditional!

Anyhow, in the midst of sweating over today's opponent and fretting about tomorrow's match, all the rikishi break into two groups, East and West (a meaningless differentiation), march single-file up to the dohyo, do one slow dignified lap, raise their arms, do a little curtsey with their sumo skirts, and march on out again.

And nobody giggles.

The yokozuna each have an individual ring-entering routine. It's more elaborate, with leg-stomping, hand-clapping, arm-lifting, and a kind of macho Japanese version of the "mashed potato"—but it all comes down to pomp and circumstance signifying nothing. This is the *Kyrie eleison*, beloved of the culture vultures, but a good time for the sports fan to slip outside for a cigarette and a leak.

The Meditations of the Beast

Once the rikishi get backstage and shed their sumo skirts, the locker room changes dramatically. Nobody says a word. Absolute silence.

"No one talks," said Shinko. "If I needed a drink, or a back rub, the younger wrestlers would have to see it in my eyes. Or sense it. And they did. I always got what I needed."

Eerie and mystical, huh?

For the student of culture unfamiliar with the universal tendency of overbearing higher-ups to expect subordinates to "read my mind," this unspoken understanding among the rikishi and their flunkies is uniquely Japanese, and the locker-room atmosphere conveys a transcendental Zen-like force. One can only conclude that it is from this preternatural silence that the rikishi must draw their strength.

For the sports fan, however, it means one thing: more tension. Here, after all, is your jock—your sumo jock. Probably a junior high school dropout with an IQ that puts him in the same range as Yogi Berra and Darryl Dawkins. Already, he's not too mentally stable, or he would have stayed in school and learned a trade. In a few minutes, he's going out in front of several thousand people to fight a guy who almost broke his neck two months ago. And he just found out that in 24 hours he's going up against a wrestler whose personal motto is: "Brain damage isn't everything. It's the only thing."

What you have here is a worried, scared, emotionally immature jock who needs to be talked to, jollied up, reassured, stroked, praised and encouraged. He needs one of the guys to chuck him upside the chin and say, "Go get 'em, Moose!" Or, "Win this one for the Gipper." Or, "This is your day, bro! That muhfuh is hist'ry." Any of those things that jocks grunt to each other. It would be nice—words of encouragement. But tradition intrudes. Instead, all of a sudden, it's church.

Ssssh.

But let's not feel too sorry. It's mean to the jocks to put them all in the deep freeze, but they get used to it. Some even like it.

Kitao/Futahaguro, for example, offered some insight into why in 1986, at the age of 22, he became one of the youngest—and craziest—rikishi ever promoted to yokozuna (only to be expelled from sumo after a violent episode two years later). "You can't stop the tension," he said, "but you can learn to enjoy it. You get yourself aroused. You know whether your opponent that day is tough, so you build up a load of hatred. If he's not so tough, you're still impatient for the match, building up confidence, looking forward to the kill. When you're really tense, people say you have to be calm, but at the same time, you have to turn yourself into a beast."

As they turn themselves into beasts, there are ways for rikishi to keep busy, to shorten the time and relieve some of the pressure. They all have to change mawashi, swab down their bods and get their hair done. And they warm up, some of them—like the Sweathog—vigorously. They dance and scowl and hyperventilate, lounge and scratch, flex and fester. Some even doze off. Naked men in church, waiting, thinking, oxidizing.

The silent society of the sumo locker room gets an athlete strangely prepared for the battle. In one sense, because he is watched and petted by his gang of pudgy acolytes, he is the center of a social whirl, a prince on a silk chaise. But in the unnatural quiet, he is also an outcast, alone with his thoughts and haunted by the infinity of simple, sudden mistakes that can ruin a sumo match, and his day, and offer him no chance for recovery.

What a difference—and probably a relief—when the rikishi steps from the wings and strides, slightly bowlegged, down the aisle to the dohyo! The arena is noisy and it smells slightly of rice and beer and yakitori. The fans are festive and other wrestlers are already on the dohyo, pawing and snorting and glaring carnivorously at each other's throats. The taut tranquility of the locker room is unique. The rikishi is like a toreador who visits the chapel in the last moment before facing the bull, only to find himself pushed incongruously into an immense saloon where drunks commune with wild animals.

The average fan sees none of this incongruity. He is oblivious, usually, to the tension, the endless waiting and recriminating that dominates sumo's backstage. The fan gets only the result; bread and circus. The real fan, however, understands the pressure that must build in so much delay, in so perverse a silence; the real fan shifts to the edge of his seat, sees behind the ample flesh of the two combatants the ratcheting of bruised nerves; and such a fan tenses also, for the inevitable. Explosion.

The explosion is called *tachiai*.

But wait. No. Not quite yet.

There are still a few inches left on the fuse.

THE SUMOTORI RAG

Pose-striking, Time-killing, and the Eight Forms of Screwing Around

Let's digress a while and drop into Shibuya, perhaps Tokyo's most fashionable consumer circus. Not far from Shibuya Station, as you weave your way patiently through a swirling plankton of post-pubescent trendiness, you'll reach a sort of hill, paved in brick and guarded at each end by shops called Loft and Ticket Saison. At the top of the hill, a saloon called the Wave Bar has cleverly planted several uncomfortable benches and a patch of foliage. Here, some of Tokyo's most self-conscious lounge lizards stand vigil for tardy companions.

Her, for instance.

Her ensemble, needless to say, shimmers. It bespeaks the toniest labels available in the city's antiseptic boutiques. Her makeup and hair are counterfeit Parisienne—a face of bone china, black eyes like the sunken stare of an infant refugee, and a scarlet wound for a mouth, a helmet of black hair that's been scalpeled just above her neo-Braque earrings. The bag, from Hermès or Carlos Falch, slouches against her thigh, half of which is impeccably nude. The other leg dangles above and supports her arms.

The arms and legs, tense in their studied repose, are the window of her demeanor—and her demeanor is her message. She leans forward, one hand a lifeless claw. In the other hand, she conducts a thin cigarette, a graceful flow that visits her lips then returns to the tableau of her blood-daubed talons. She leans her head back to exhale smoke, in a thin stream that—incongruously—brings to mind a factory whistle at lunchtime. Her leaden eyelids overstate her ennui just enough (shades of Theda Bara) to ensure that the hayseeds in the back row don't miss the drift. It's barely possible to catch the flicker of her pupils as she glimpses to see if anyone (please, someone!) notices. To stare at her affords rich gratification, because in return you can feel the electric rush she gets from attention.

She is a living cameo of that singular Tokyo type: the virgin vamp.

And him?

He has spread-eagled his calfskin legs outward, and passersby must step high that they don't nick one of his hand-tooled Buck Owens boots and hit the bricks face-first. The jacket is also leather—mauve, cut to the waist and fastened there, but open above to display the shirt and tie—pastels coordinated, by rote, with the other components. The hair is a raven coiffure, sustained by mousse, that defies gravity, centrifugal force and gale-force winds (but might be inflammable). It cants outward, spikes upward, glistens weirdly in the presence of neon, and turns his silhouette into something resembling the carcass of a mangled arthropod.

Again, though, you must observe his angle of repose. He has spread his hands wide behind, so that his body forms, roughly, a bent "X." The inevitable cigarette smolders between two fingers, and he stabs it at his mouth in regular, surly thrusts. His lip curls, Bogart-style, with each painful drag. He doesn't exhale, exactly, but lets the smoke seep between his parted lips and wreathe his face. As he waits, his restless gaze scans, pauses, examines, scans again. Here is Joe Cool, awaiting his main squeeze but alert just in case, ready to improvise if a more interesting prospect crosses his path.

At the right hour of a Friday night, the Wave Bar benches exhibit a steady relay of poseurs, in a panoply of costumes, in an array of roles that would inspire a Brecht—each of them delectably, theatrically aloof.

The tableau always crumbles, when the date—or very often, the group—arrives, turning erstwhile James Deans and Charlotte Ramplings back into antic Japanese adolescents. Watching the vigil, at the Wave Bar, or at Almond in Roppongi, or in front of the San-Ai Building in Ginza, is like being caught in a mass screen test—because Japan, especially Tokyo, is the world capital of pose-striking. No group of young people on earth—not even Paris or L.A.—is quite so stylish, so slavish in adherence to the

written instructions dispensed in the fashion magazines. No population Does and Doesn't so religiously
their Glamor "Do's and Don't's," nor is so aware of the
proper physical attitude necessary to exhibition of
the costly threads that serve as the uniforms of each
peer group.

Pose-striking in Japan, whether intentional or
instinctual, expresses both ego and group absorption.
Even though one does not—wisely—reject attachment to some group, there is consolation in choosing
one's subgroup, deciding in which little repertory
company you prefer to do your role-playing. Pose-
striking is, simultaneously, the escape from the
group to which one must belong, and the signature of
the group to which one wants to belong. It defines
one's identity, in equal measure, in a kabuki troupe
or a motorcycle gang. The point, at bottom, is not to
be an "original," as it might be in the West, but to be
an archetype.

The Importance of the Overture

Sumo wrestlers, of course, live by the pose. From
the moment the rikishi leaves the silent sweatbox of
the locker room and strides down the aisle toward the
dohyo, he joins a slow-motion tango of pose-striking.
In his three to five minutes before tachiai, he portrays
himself—with all eyes on him and no hand
controlling him—not as he is, but in his version of
how an ideal athlete ought to be. He strives toward
the essence of sumo, the archetype of his fraternity.
The prematch performance of the rikishi, his
personal overture, is an eloquent set of poses,
because it is both contrived and unconscious,
because the rikishi springs from one of the most

rigid, disciplined and hypnotic subcultures in a rigid, disciplined and hypnotized nation.

For every sumo match, for every rikishi in, at least, this century, every movement in the overture has been the same, preordained. Every rikishi who makes it to the bigtime is an honor graduate of the Hollyhock & Calabash Academy of Terpsichory. Except, ah, you can't force every little thing. These are jocks—big dumb, immature, sheltered guys with overwrought egos—and you have to give them all some room to get ready, each according to his own drummer. The Sumotori Rag has, unavoidably, a million variations.

This is not, however, immediately apparent. To the Western eye, these overtures—every bloody match!—seem endless, pointless, interesting a few times but eventually tedious (even if you insist that you just love Japanese rituals) unless . . .

. . . Unless you know the rikishi.

You can't cancel the Sumotori Rag. You cannot fast-forward to the action, because if you did that, the match would be lifeless. You would reduce the rikishi to eternal ciphers and the drama to little more than noises from the pigsty. The overture is where, in all the apparently senseless wandering and stomping, clapping and scowling, posing and screwing around, you find the personality of the rikishi, the imp beneath the archetype, the boy beneath the blubber.

Here's how it happens.

The rikishi steps forth from the proscenium and waddles down the aisle several matches before his own. The crowd is inches away on both sides, and when the rikishi sits down beside one of the five ring judges to await his match, he is literally part of the audience. Sumo has no dugouts, bullpens, player's box or foul territory. However, the rikishi is comfy, because he sits on a ridiculously plump cushion— his very own personal pillow—that has been set in place ahead of his arrival by one of the elves from his sumobeya. As the rikishi awaits his match, he poses. His legs are crossed. His arms are either (a) crossed belligerently and nestled on the bulge of his belly or (b) planted on his knees. Unless one or both of the behemoths fighting up on the dohyo threaten to land on him, he holds that pose until he is called. Sometimes he is so engrossed in that pose that he doesn't—or can't—move out of the way in time. Once, Fujinoshin froze so stoically in his ringside pose that he himself became the landing strip for a flying rikishi. While his pose-striking may have been commendable, having to default the rest of the basho with a broken ankle was idiotic.

Normally, the rikishi only moves when the ref (*gyoji*) hollers for him. The ref himself is a genius of pose-striking. A ref who can't deck himself out and stiffen his back like a tourist-shop geisha doll never moves up from the minor leagues. The ref's costume (traditional, of course) is . . . well, some outfits defy description. Suffice to say that if Liberace and Salvador Dali had gotten together to design sleepwear for the Phashionable Pharisee, their inspiration would have probably fallen short of the frippery in which your typical sumo ref minces about the dohyo. To bestir the rikishi from ringside, the ref holds out his indispensable "war fan" (*goombai*) and passes it over each rikishi as he announces the wrestlers' (a) names, (b) sumobeya, and (c) home prefectures—in a bone-jangling squall that would put him into the hog-calling finals, at 6–5 for the title, at any county fair in Arkansas. The ref's pose, complete with the Peter Max peignoir, is medieval, florid, silly and superb. It presents a luscious contrast to the rikishi's nudity. Also, the ref's ecclesiastical solemnity, underscored by the nail-on-blackboard ring announcement, is a sharp reminder that most sumo fans still aren't sure whether this is High Mass or a Tijuana cockfight.

Finally, the rikishi clamber up the steps and onto the dohyo. They begin their overture. From the first movements, everything is scripted. Officially, there are six distinct steps in the Sumotori Rag, after each of which the rikishi return to their corners and pick up a handful of salt, which they toss before themselves (purifying the ground) as they step back onto the dohyo. The official movements, in their usual order, are:

1) The entrance ritual. Back to back, they face each other.

2) The spitting, screaming ritual. While the rikishi drink holy water, spit it out and then wipe their mouths with holy paper, the ref screams their names.

3) The stomping ritual, in which they face each other, clap their hands, lift each leg in turn and stomp the dohyo. They do this twice, once from a distance, once at the center of the dohyo.

4) The shuffling ritual, in which they paw the sand with their feet.

5) The squatting ritual, which they perform three, four or five times—depending on rank. They squat

and check each other out, lean forward and touch their fists to the sand, then return to their squat, stand and go back to the corner. This ritual offers many opportunities for ad-libbing.

6) Finally, tachiai.

"Kokoro" and KTUSH

Needless to say, these basic steps are only the skeleton of the rich and varied screwing around that precedes the match. Sumo nerds aver that this period (as short as a minute, as long as six minutes) of the Sumotori Rag is one of the most "uniquely Japanese" of all sumo's features. This assertion is harmless and romantic, and simplistic enough to carry a measure of truth. It's especially attractive for those who cherish sumo mainly because it evokes that ineffable throbbing within Japanese culture which the natives call *"kokoro."* This is a word that, of course, they insist is untranslatable but which seems nicely covered by the concept of "soul."

The truly distinctive feature, actually, in the pre-tachiai overture is that it epitomizes the Japanese talent for expressing individuality while falling in with one's group. It is the canticle of the Pose.

By the same token, the pre-tachiai screwing around is readily familiar to any observant sports fan. For instance, go to a few track meets and watch the sprinters shaking their legs, and go to a football game and check out the linemen running into each other's helmets and pounding shoulder pads, and go to a baseball game and watch as all the players carry on their own tiresome rituals of chewing, spitting, cleat-tapping, juggling the resin bag, adjusting their caps and hitching up their gonads.

No difference. It all comes under the rubric of Killing Time Until Something Happens (KTUSH). The beauty of sumo is that the match itself contains no KTUSH whatsoever. Compare soccer, if you will—the world's most popular game—in which most games end in scoreless ties, so that the 90 minutes of regulation play, and a half-hour of "extra time," serve mainly as prelude to the ridiculous tie-breaker shootout that finally decides the game.

Most of American football consists of KTUSH— huddles and communiqués from the sidelines. Too much basketball is wasted on timeouts, free throws, guys lying on the floor with sprained ankles and undergraduate volunteers wiping sweat off the floor after the guys with the sprained ankles get carried away. And don't forget baseball, in which the stretch position is a microcosm of the each game's entire three hours of suspense, and/or sleep (depending on your point of view).

In sumo, at least, KTUSH has an honored role. It's part of the game, and nobody ever talks about ways to reduce the screwing around and speed up the action. The prescribed rituals—as in other sports— serve the jocks as an energy release and a kind of self-hypnosis. For each rikishi, the pre-tachiai pose-striking is an unconscious routine. "If I noticed what I was doing, if I noticed something different," said former sekitori Shinko, "I knew I was in trouble."

Kitao/Futahaguro echoed Shinko's explanation. "Once you're on the dohyo, you think of nothing," he said. "You empty your mind. You operate only on your built-up confidence, and you forget the battle plan. Your body has to remember, automatically, what to do. If you start thinking now, you're dead meat."

This self-hypnosis is the reason, I suspect, why a rikishi is not ready for the bigtime until he has devised his very own Rag. It's a groove you have to find before you can comfortably walk beneath a spotlight with your clothes off, in front of 11,000 people (not to mention a national TV audience) and charge head-first into a 300-pound psychotic cretin with hands like cinder blocks.

The KTUSH Pecking Order

KTUSH in sumo, thus justified, has its standard rituals. But within these movements, the rikishi extemporize subtly, artistically, infinitely. Always in Japan, within the group forms, there are private forms of screwing around. It is in these personal poses and flourishes that rikishi offer their messages to the world; they signify the encroachment of tachiai and the texture of the impending clash. It is here that the fan refines his appreciation of sumo's overtures, of sumo itself.

Screwing around before the match is a privilege a rikishi must earn. The higher your rank, the more KTUSH you get. The lowest-level makushita matches are little more than wham-bam-thank-you-ma'am, with the wrestlers hustled on and off the dohyo at little more than 60 seconds a pop. In makushita, the referees wear simpler nighties and go barefoot, and the wrestlers don't get a saltbox to play with. They wear grubby old brown mawashi and they don't have any hairdressing privileges. Instead of 15 matches in a basho, the scrubs only get seven matches to prove themselves.

A novice nun, or a first-year seminarian, would understand the life of a makushita wrestler. Life sucks, and then you pray.

It is in the preliminary matches that the fan learns to appreciate the aristocratic elegance and leisurely melodrama that attends the longer, loftier matches.

In the two upper divisions, which come complete with bright belts, saltboxes, flunkies, and a personal washcloth for every rikishi, the differences in rank are defined by the duration of KTUSH. In the second division—juryo—matches, each wrestler gets about three minutes to shuffle, flex and scratch his nuts. I've timed the matches, and recorded a KTUSH range between 2:50 and 3:25.

In the lower levels of the upper, makuuchi, division, from the bottom maegashira all the way up to sekiwake (the third highest rank), rikishi are permitted minimum KTUSH of 3:20, and nobody asks questions if they take as long as 3:50. Among the two top ranks, ozeki and yokozuna, screwing around is an art form. This is where delay takes on shades and permutations that would win an admiring nod from C. Northcote Parkinson. The fastest ozeki/yokozuna match in this century might have gotten off in three minutes and fifty seconds. Four minutes is really fast, and most ozeki/ yokozuna clashes offer around five minutes of KTUSH.

The grand master of screwing around before the match, however—no contest—is Konishiki the Hawaiian hippo. Chiyonofuji, for example, was an efficient, no-nonsense screwer-around, who normally got to tachiai in 4:40. But when he wrestled Konishiki—who always sets the pace—the time dragged on to around 5:50. Konishiki is the only rikishi to break the six-minute Sumotori Rag. His strategy is apparent and convincing. When you

weight 500 pounds, it is a wise policy to make your opponent look as long as possible at that 500 pound whopping, swollen, bulging, thrusting, drooping, shivering, quaking, monstrous, hostile paunch, and think about them before slamming head-first into the pile and trying to get ahold of it.

Kunishili either lets off his malaise by just sitting there. His poise is a dangling one. He seems to grow before your eyes.

Eight Ways to Screw Around...

Someone's talent in KTUSH says much for his ganut. Few rituals, as ... as he does ... basic forms of screwing around comprising the sand-shuffling, self-picking finger-licking, the self-abuse, and jump-jumping. Several techniques are part of the standard one's dealt with by the Sumo; and finally some of the variations and some ... important to ... To the ... to distinguish these moves, here is some KTUSH Lore.

(1) STOMPING: This is the all-too-familiar start the Rag, to lift one's foot all the way off the ground. This is called an Ili.

Shiko dates back at least to early 17th century, and is a part of a book which illustrates originally meant to show that the ninja is one tough bambino even with his clothes off, can be poured to overpass. The modern ritualism that abounds sumo stomping, however, is far more ...

Every time we discuss sumo Junko's pet litany, reminiscing that shiko is one of the greatest exercises ever invented. It is also robust health and vitality ...

weigh 500 pounds, it is a wise policy to make your opponent look as long as possible at that 500 great whopping, swollen, bulging, bursting, drooping, shivering, crushing, monstrous, hostile pounds, and think about them before smashing head-first into the pile and trying to get ahold of it.

Konishiki wins a lot of his matches by just sitting there. His pose is a bludgeon. He seems to grow before your eyes.

Eight Ways to Screw Around

Konishiki's talent for KTUSH runs the proverbial gamut. Few rikishi use, as well as he does, the eight basic forms of screwing around: stomping, squatting, sand-shuffling, salt-pitching, finger-licking, staring, self-abuse, and armpit-wiping. Some of these techniques are part of the standard overture set forth by the Sumo Association, some are expansions and variations, and some are unauthorized. To help you to distinguish these nuances, here is some KTUSH Lore.

1) STOMPING. The rikishi are all required, as they start the Rag, to lift each leg in turn and stomp it on the ground. This is called *shiko*.

Shiko dates back at least to the 17th century, and it's part of a buck-and-wing that was originally meant to show that the rikishi is one tough sumbitch even with his clothes off and no concealed weapons. The modern mystique that surrounds sumo stomping, however, is far more curious.

Every time we discuss sumo, Junko's pal, Hitomi, reminds me that shiko is one of the greatest exercises in the world. It bestows robust health and demonstrates a level of agility that would dwarf (if that's possible) Mary Lou Retton. I always nod indulgently, because Hitomi is a true believer in shiko. She—like millions of others—has been won over by propagandists who proselytize far and wide the restorative magic of sumo stomping. It beats the hell out of tai chi, yoga, dancercise, even oat bran!

I have realized that it lies neither in the power nor province of one agnostic gaijin to uproot this faith. The reason for the local devotion to this rather ungainly leg-lifting act, I think, is that shiko is the rebuttal to all those skeptics who insist that sumo isn't a real sport because the players are all fat, out-of-breath and chronically dyspeptic.

"A lot you know," retorts the true believer. "These guys may not be built like Michelangelo's David, but answer me this: Could Michelangelo's David do shiko?"

A pretty devastating rejoinder . . . except, well, yeah, if he wasn't a statue, David could do shiko. Easy.

I can do shiko. My mom can do it. Konishiki, f'Chrissake—500 pounds of dangerous, unsightly fat—he does it every day. It's a simple exercise. It doesn't require any sort of conditioning. It takes about ten minutes to learn how to do it as niftily as a 20-year sumo veteran. It's not aerobic, not anaerobic, not even much of a strain until you hit about 15 reps. And sumo wrestlers don't do reps. It ain't dignified.

There is some evidence to support the assertion that sumo stomping does indicate a certain flexibility around the hips and groin, but this probably derives not so much from shiko as from the standard

Japanese toilet stance—which requires a deep, deep knee-bend over a hole in the floor, and accounts for Japan's incredibly high incidence of hemorrhoids.

The actual, honest beauty of sumo stomping, and the reason I love it despite its uselessness, is that it looks so good. It's a wonderful pose, and I think the world would be a happier, healthier, sillier place if everybody—before they head for the bar and start talking property values—would face off for a congenial session of leg-lifting and foot-stomping.

Naturally, each rikishi has his own shiko. The young, athletic rikishi tend to emphasize elevation and a powerful finish. The whales prefer to stay low and affect a worldly disdain.

2) SQUATTING. Squatting is the soul of the Sumotori Rag. At the highest levels, each rikishi in each match has to squat at least eight times. During the squatting ritual, each squat is actually a double-squat—because the wrestlers both lean forward into a four-point stance, returning to the squat before standing again.

Because the squat is the most complicated form of KTUSH in sumo, it invites creativity. It is in his squat that Konishiki extends his matches. He descends slowly, lingers majestically and ascends deliberately. While deep in his squat, he assumes a pose that he has—in a way—claimed as his signature. On his right knee his right paw, on his left knee his left elbow—so that Konishiki cants the awesome brown bod slightly to the left. He looks—yes! Rakish.

Others use this pose, the Hawaiian Tilt, but no one with such intimidating panache. My favorite variation, in recent years, has been demonstrated by a middling (but lovable) maegashira named Tochi-tsukasa. He begins with the standard squat, but you notice right away how deep he sinks. His ass almost brushes the floor. Then he leans into the four-point stance, squats back, and for a wonderful moment, you think maybe Tochitsukasa is stuck. He can't stand all that weight up again! He rocks back and forth like a Land Rover axle-deep in an elephant wallow. In the meantime, he poses his arms in a "praying mantis," his elbows inside his knees.

No, he isn't stuck! This is theater. The rocking accelerates, his fists tighten, his face twists into a lemon-sucking scowl, and then, thrusting his forearms forward once more and slapping the outside of his knees, his last hipswivel brings him upright again. He stalks back to his corner. The fans go wild.

The Goldfish (Ozutsu) does a variation called the "duck landing." His squat is tense, and as he rises, his elbows are outside his knees, his short arms almost straight, and his fists aimed at the floor—just about the way a duck spreads its wings down as it's about to hit the pond. Akinoshima, a mean, short, strong wrestler, grinds his fists into the sand, then brandishes his fists and forearms in a much more threatening "praying mantis" than Tochitsukasa's.

Tamakairiki, a juryo who might never make makuuchi, affects the Hawaiian Tilt and also bounces incessantly during the faceoff. Tochinowaka, whose shoulders are massive, combines "praying mantis" and "duck landing." Masurao, an injury-prone but classy veteran who had to retire in 1990, avoided touching the dohyo during all the preliminary squats—putting his hands to the ground only at tachiai.

And so it goes. A squat, to the untrained eye, is only a squat. By the same token, the fair-weather fan couldn't tell the difference between Juan Marichal's delivery and Bruce Hurst's pickoff move.

3) SAND-SHUFFLING. Before the first complete squat-and-faceoff, the two rikishi resemble a couple of baseball hitters, kicking the dirt around the batter's box. They watch their feet, roll their shoulders, clutch their belts, and try to look casually menacing. Some make semicircles in the sand, some draw lines, some barely disturb the dirt—just look at it with an air of pensiveness. But this always: Only when they get into the squat do they deign to acknowledge one another.

Thereafter, all the sand-shuffling occurs in their strolls to the saltbox and back. The variations are infinite. Hokutoumi, the frightening yokozuna, is the master of the "robot walk," a stiff-legged gait that suggests that his pent-up, psychotic fury is barely contained. The Sweathog (Fujinoshin) has a habit of dragging his toes on the sand as he rises from the squat and turns toward the saltbox.

Hananofuji, a perennial juryo, pounds his heels as he heads for the corner, and Konishiki—always the innovator—gets the sand off his feet by tapping them on the backs of his calves.

A seasoned sumo fan knows his rikishi just by watching their feet.

4) SALT-PITCHING. After they attend funerals and

before they re-enter their houses, Japanese people perpetuate a Shinto belief in salt as a symbol of purification, by sprinkling it on their doorsteps. The salt prevents the contagion of death from clinging to them within their homes. Thus, salt in the sumo ring poetically kills germs, whitens the path of the rikishi, and banishes the specter of past defeats.

I doubt that any rikishi thinks of all this rustic sorcery as he marches forth and back in a day of sumo. And the only fans who think this way are the gaijin rubes who are still bogged down in Cultural Appreciation.

Salt-pitching is the most picturesque moment in the Sumotori Rag. Check through any sumo guide or an issue of *Sumo World*. Half the rikishi portraits depict the jocks spreading purification before themselves. None of the standard lore, however, discusses methods of salt-pitching—a shameful omission because this is the instant when all the fans momentarily pause, rest their chopsticks, freeze the beer glass on their lips, and peer at the dohyo.

Then two portions of salt mingle in the air, the rikishi step forth, the ref twirls his goombai, the fans burp, the rikishi face off . . . the moment passes. But it always comes around again, strange and fascinating and artful.

There are three basic deliveries for salt-pitching, the underhand, the sidearm and the flip. Lately, the flip seems most popular, but fashion is notoriously fickle. The sidearm delivery, for instance, currently enjoys a rising vogue because Chiyonofuji—the most influential stylist of our time—brought it from the third-base side.

No two rikishi pitch salt exactly alike, because

variations occur in such areas as wrist-action (an inward twist, an outward twist, no twist at all), volume and elevation of salt, and follow-through.

Hokutoumi, for instance, throws underhand, with an inward twist, moderate volume, elevation slightly high (just above eye level), and a moderate follow-through. He is the classic conservative salt pitcher—which is appropriate to his lofty station. The power of Hokutoumi's salt routine lies in his face, where an air of hostility suggests that he is spreading not salt, but a mixture of broken glass and the ground-up bones of his victims.

Kushimaumi (Stretch) entered the makuuchi lists with a refined salt delivery, learned from four years of stellar intercollegiate sumo. He's a sidearmer, doesn't throw a lot of salt and doesn't get any elevation (sidearmers rarely do). But an early release and a sweeping follow-through create a distinctive motion. Kushimaumi, in almost every aspect of the Sumotori Rag, is one of the prettiest stylists to emerge in the last decade. He moves like three or four Fred Astaires (apparently after having eaten Ginger Rogers for lunch).

Asahifuji, like Hokutoumi, understates everything and adds emphasis with the malevolence of his gaze. He flips, with a slight inward twist, light volume, moderate elevation and minimum follow-through. He's elegant, but dull. Much more interesting among flippers is Kirinishiki, who puts mustard on the old salt, gives his delivery lots of wrist, with moderate elevation and a tight follow-through. But the nice part is that he stands there on the tawara for an appreciative moment, watching his salt arc upward and array itself on the sand—as though reading portent in its pattern of distribution.

Little Spoon, Takahanada, is a flipper who seems intentionally devoid of style or flourish, hiding a swelled head behind a mask of modesty. But he has one rare distinction. He's a southpaw.

As of 1990, Tamakairiki was the only rikishi in sumo with an overhand delivery, dashing the salt at his feet in a hard spray. Trashcan (Ryogoku) is also a watcher. Konishiki dribbles.

No discussion of salt-pitching, however, is adequate without a description of Mitoizumi's routine. It is from his salt-pitching extravagance that he has earned our affectionate nickname, "The Asshole." In all but his final pitch, Mitoizumi's delivery is less than desultory. He picks up barely a pinch of salt, then discards it carelessly, flipping it away from himself, with no wrist English.

Needless to say, this careless attitude is a pose. Mitoizumi comes out for his final pitch like Evel Knievel hitting the wall of fire. The Asshole empties the saltbox into his paw, spins toward the dohyo, swings back his pitching arm and then launches the whole four-pound handful, ten meters into the air, in a slow-pitch softball underhand that creates a cloudburst of salt. Mitoizumi tramples every standard of athletic forebearance and good taste, and he receives, in return, a joyful round of oohs, ahs and giggles from the middle-aged ladies in the audience, very few of whom have ever had an orgasm or seen Wayne Newton Live. Mitoizumi is an unintentional, sophomoric troublemaker and his fans love it.

Occasionally, his juvenile salt act even helps the

Asshole. The rikishi who watches, and reacts to Mitoizumi's preposterous display is just distracted enough to be easy pickings at tachiai. I've seen Trashcan lose a match to the Asshole solely because he paused to roll his eyes at the sight of Mitoizumi's descending salt storm. It was a break in concentration that foreshadowed defeat.

5) FINGER-LICKING. Compared to squatting and salt-throwing, finger-licking is a minor feature of the Sumotori Rag. Some rikishi lick salt from their fingers for good luck. Many don't even bother. Sumo wrestlers who finger-lick are like the white basketball players at Holy Cross who make the sign of the cross at the free-throw line.

Usually, rikishi try to do their finger-licking as quickly and daintily as possible (except Mitoizumi, who hits himself in the face and laps his palm like a Rottweiler in an Alpo commercial). Walking up to tachiai with a sudden overdose of salt (and the accompanying urge to spit it out and get a drink of water) is the sort of distraction that cancels the salt's dubious felicity.

6) STARING. Looking bullets, daggers and ICBMs at your opponent is probably the most outright entertaining step in the Sumotori Rag—which is, of course, why it invites the censure of the old farts in the Sumo Association (who all used to do it themselves).

The most prominent anti-staring decree came just prior to the May Basho of 1990, when Futagoyama, Old Fart Number One (head of the Sumo Association), announced that Konishiki's trademark staring contests were *Hin ga nai* ("Tacky, tacky, tacky!"). Futa-goyama's announcement was duly leaked to the weekly press—so that the public would know that Konishiki's wrists had been slapped. Konishiki, for his part, knew that his chances for promotion to yokozuna rested not just on his performance on the dohyo, but on his willingness to cramp his crowd-pleasing style by bowing to the head honcho of sumo. It was as if Pete Rozelle had banned Mark Gastineau's sack dance, or David Stern ordered Michael Jordan to stop wearing Bermuda shorts and sticking out his tongue.

Konishiki complied, robbing sumo of a wonderful moment. But before the Old Fart got to him, Konishiki would linger in each of his pre-tachiai squats, mountainously inert in his Hawaiian Tilt, glaring murderously at his foe and waiting, forcing the other guy—always—to look away first. Konishiki's staredowns are moments of universal empathy. The fan instinctively participates in that silent war of wills. Guys have been working on their stares since Ogg took on Alley Oop for dibs on Raquel Welch. Konishiki's glare is the same staring contest that has preceded every playground scuffle since the invention of recess. It is the same staring contest that drives fight fans to frenzy just before the main event. It is Jack Palance, in *Shane,* looking down from the loading dock into Elisha Cook's rabbit eyes, and waiting—waiting for the poor dumb sodbuster to make the first move and seal his bloody fate.

Konishiki's staring contest is a legend, and a weapon. It drags out the Sumotori Rag, alters the other rikishi's rhythm, diverts energy from fighting to showing off. It makes every other wrestler feel a little bit like Elisha Cook. Tochinowaka, another epic starer, is almost mesmerized by Konishiki. And Hokutoumi—whose pyschopathic glower is the only stare more horrible than Konishiki's—nearly flinches when he brushes eyeballs with Konishiki. Only a few rikishi, Chiyonofuji among them, refused to engage Konishiki in the Great Stare. Among jocks, any challenge as overt as this is irresistible. To back off is to abandon the pose that places you among the jock brotherhood.

Among those who were angered at Futagoyama's ban was Shinko, a devout follower of almost all of sumo's rules, but also a fan of Konishiki and a connoisseur of pizzazz. "Every rikishi has to express his own style," said Shinko. "Konishiki was just getting ready in his own way, and the fans really liked it."

However, all this controversy aside, the Old Fart's ban was a passing ripple. Staring is more intrinsic to modern sumo than squatting or chankonabe, and it will reassert itself completely by the time this book is published. When done well by two rikishi with a flair for the stare, it's a crescendo that starts with a glance, proceeds to a look, advances to a scowl and ascends in the last faceoff to a glacial glower of vaudevillian loathing. It is beautiful, demented, histrionic and—at best—it seems to go on forever and ever. It is the height of The Pose. The great staring contests prompt spontaneous applause and nervous laughter, simultaneously and contagiously, among the 11,000 fans in the Ryogoku Kokugikan. And at home, they inspire the couch potato to summon his mate, shouting excitedly, "Hey, c'mere, check this out. Quick! They're gonna kill each other."

7) SELF-ABUSE. As the countdown nears its end, rikishi will start hitting themselves on the face and thighs, slapping their ass and thumping their mawashi. The last thirty seconds before tachiai sounds vaguely like rutting season among bighorn rams in the High Sierra. But the secretion reaching critical mass at this moment is not testosterone but adrenaline.

In team sports, you can always count on your teammates to high-five, low-five and elbow-bang you to a fare-thee-well, rub your shoulders, tousle your hair, bash your helmet, abuse your pads and rub your ass 'til it's rosy-red—at which point your adrenaline is high enough to send you through a concrete wall without pain.

Sumo, however, is one of the loneliest sports in the world. Even the guys on your side—the pudgy elves who hover behind you, carry your pillow and wait in the wings with your bathrobe—are forbidden from laying comradely hands on you. In sumo, if you don't abuse yourself into a wild-eyed, slobbering frenzy, ain't nobody gonna do it for ya.

As usual, the foremost self-abuser is the Asshole, who—throughout the Sumotori Rag—whales away at his decorator-colored mawashi and pummels his tochis, and then lets it all hang out after the last faceoff. He takes a big drink of water and sprays it all over his feet. He slaps his legs, throws enough salt to preserve this month's North Pacific salmon catch and then charges onto to the dohyo hitting himself in the face.

Sometimes it works, sometimes it doesn't, but who cares? Hit yourself again, big guy!

8) ARMPIT-WIPING. Mitoizumi is frantic and fun, but for all that screwing around, his Sumotori Rag is inefficient. He fails often, because he works harder at The Pose than at the job.

By comparison, Chiyonofuji's Rag was almost invisible. His pose enhanced his art. He prepared himself with unwavering consistency, and a coldblooded economy of energy. Nothing altered, nothing wasted. It was Chiyonofuji whom I always watched most intently through the Rag. I always knew, in his matches, when tachiai was nigh— because of the pink washcloth.

Each rikishi brings a washcloth (*oshibori*) to his match. It's kept by the ringside flunky, who offers it to him after the last faceoff before tachiai. Some (Chiyonofuji, Hokutoumi, the Sweathog) accept it; some (Asahifuji, Kirishima) disdain the washcloth. Those who use it, swab themselves off manfully— concentrating on the face, the chest, lastly of course, the pits. Hokutoumi's washcloth routine is especially distinctive. He shrugs his shoulders and looks into the washcloth before immersing his face—like a contestant in a life-or-death apple-bob.

For the fan, the important aspect of armpit-wiping is that it signals tachiai. When Chiyo takes the pink washcloth from the fat kid in the corner and swabs himself off, the Rag is over. Put down your newspaper. It's time to boogie.

Dumb fans will probably never appreciate the Sumotori Rag, because they don't understand that sumo is largely psychological. Concentration wins matches—more than muscle, more than finesse, more than memorizing all the silly names for every throw. A great rikishi spends that five minutes before the match tightening his focus to the point where he wouldn't recognize his own mother if she handed him a baby-blue washcloth, pinched his cheek and said, "Kick ass, sonny!"

Screwing around. If you love it, you're a fan. If you don't, you're a seat number.

TACHIAI

Hookers, Bulldozers, Boxers, Stranglers, Matadors, and Lowdown Yankee Liars

"You're a lowdown Yankee liar."

"Prove it."

Thus, Elisha Cook as the hot-tempered farmer challenges Jack Palance, the hired gun, in *Shane*. The next few seconds provide one of film history's most beautifully poignant scenes. Cook, angry, terrified and spoiling for a fight, goes for his gun, only to hear—he doesn't even *see*—Palance's lightning draw. Cook is still looking at his holster, like a bad basketball player watching himself dribble, while Palance's six-shooter is leveled at his heart. He waits, frozen.

In director George Stevens' tragic parody of all the thousands of movie gunfights ever filmed, Cook lifts his Colt slowly, hopelessly, still averting his gaze from the killer's dead eyes. Palance ends the torture abruptly. One shot flings the overmatched farmer dead, into the mud.

Later in the movie, Alan Ladd (Shane), of course, reverses the drama, facing Palance in Grafton's Saloon and waiting him out. He forces Palance to draw first and blasts him . . . into the pickle barrel and Kingdom Come.

Great, stirring stuff—now a relic of the past. Old West and old movies. Except in Japan, folks! For sumo is the last refuge of the "quick draw." Sumo reenacts the tension of the classic Western showdown every day of every basho—200 times a day and 3,000 times every tournament (give or take a few matches). How so? Because every tachiai—the moment that two rikishi burst from their last squat into a clash of muscle, flab, sand and hair grease—has more in common with a Wild West gunfight than any faceoff in any other modern professional sport. Sumo, unlike every other popular sport, requires its competitors to start themselves—like Cook and Palance waiting each other out beneath the brooding Teton skies. There's no whistle, no starting gun, no tip-off, nobody to drop the puck, and no goddamn blind ump to holler "Play ball."

The ref is there, of course, resplendent in his lavender taffeta frock and flourishing his shiny goombai, but all he says is "On your mark . . . get set . . . "

The "go" is left up to the jocks. They squat, they glare, they sweat, they wait. They "breathe together." Their hands—in Elisha Cook slow-motion—descend toward the sand. Ideally, the drop of the hands occurs in synchrony, and when both rikishi brush the dohyo with two—not one! Two—hands, they lunge at one another simultaneously.

Ideally.

Sure.

In 79 percent of all sumo matches, according to a highly reliable independent study done by me, one rikishi draws first. He disdains the "ideal" and tries to get the jump on his opponent. Futagoyama, the Sumo Association fossil who polices the fat guys, tries to enforce the notion that every tachiai is—or at least oughta be—dead even. He should shut up. He's pissing into the typhoon.

Jumpers and Receivers

When I understood, after a year or so of watching sumo, the intent of tachiai—as defined by ideologues like Futagoyama—compared to the reality of tachiai— one guy grabbing a split-second edge on the other— I wondered if it mattered either way. I supposed, at first—one always supposes—that the guy with the jump (the Jumper) gains a tiny, but crucial advantage over the guy who starts late (the Receiver).

But the evidence of other sports immediately argued against this supposition. Carl Lewis, for instance—the sprinter of the '80s—is a notoriously slow starter. He avers that he derives extra motivation from his tardy starts, because he can see the field of runners in front of him. He knows what he must do, how hard he must push, how far he must go to catch up.

Theoretically, the evidence provided by Elisha Cook, Alan Ladd, Jack Palance, James Arness, Gary Cooper, Quick Draw McGraw, and many others, support the Lewis proposition, that the Receiver—

armed with desperation—has the real edge over the Jumper.

But Carl Lewis might simply be alibiing his lone athletic deficiency. And really, Marv, how can you trust gunfight data, when the only documentation you have comes from Hollywood scriptwriters who ultimately have to kill the Bad Guy and reinforce the one absolute code of the Western movie: Good Guys never draw first?

Wait, wait! There's proof.

Receivers beat Jumpers. It's true. We even have data . . .

Sort of.

OK, so I don't have it on me. So maybe it's apocryphal. I still believe it.

Besides, it's fun.

You see, when I was a kid, I read this article about Neils Bohr, the Nobel Prize physicist, the one who helped conceptualize the atom bomb. Remember?

Well, Bohr, it seems, was nuts about Western movies. He watched hundreds of Westerns. Eventually, the same question occurred to Neils Bohr that strikes everyone as they watch their 4,065th shootout. Is it just a Hollywood convention that the (usually Bad) guy who draws first tends to lose, or are such results a true depiction of physical, scientific reality? Neils Bohr wanted to know. He was, after all, a scientist. He did not rest easy in the presence of an unsolved conundrum.

But how to solve it?

He couldn't restore the Wild West, and he lived in an era prior to the emergence of Michael J. Fox and Christopher Lloyd, so Neils Bohr did the next best thing. He ordered everyone working in his nuclear physics lab (in Denmark, by the way) to strap toy six-guns onto their hips. He told them that, every time they met in the corridor, they should slap leather and draw, blast away at each other and then record the results.

The results, at least according to this possibly apocryphal and blatantly unverifiable tale I read when I was a child—which, incidentally, turned me into a Neils Bohr fan for life—strongly supported the surprising conclusion that (all other factors being equal [which they never are]) a Receiver will consistently beat a Jumper. Bohr's subsequent hypothesis was that, in seeing the Jumper go for his gun, the Receiver receives a stimulus—a mental message that screams "HURRY!"—and an accompanying rush of adrenaline that wipes out his instant of hesitation and sends the Jumper, that lowdown Yankee liar, to Boot Hill.

Bohr's Constant vs. The Human Factor

Tachiai is the same—the only modern parallel to the now-defunct Wild West gunfight. Only through sumo can we even remotely relive those thrilling days of yesteryear—AND—duplicate Neils Bohr's break-through research in gunslingin'.

Which I've done.

I studied 17 days of sumo, in two basho in 1990, running videotape backward and forward in slow-motion 'til I was cross-eyed, through 443 tachiai, in the juryo and makuuchi divisions. Of this total, 117 tachiai—26 percent—were either dead even or were not relevant to the outcome of the match.

In the remaining 326 tachiai, one rikishi got the jump, sometimes infinitesimal but discernible. The

Jumpers won 134 matches (41 percent), the Receivers won 192 (59 percent). Of the 17 days I studied, Receivers dominated Jumpers 15 times, with one victory for the Jumpers and one day tied.

Ergo? Bohr's Constant applies to sumo. The guy who draws first—in almost six cases out of ten—bites the dust.

My results supported my expectations, but they also undermined them. Several purely human factors mitigate against this largely mechanical analysis.

For instance, the truly second-rate rikishi who gains an advantage in tachiai is likely to waste it immediately with his next dumb move.

Second, the significance of tachiai decreases with the length of the match. In any match that runs beyond 30 seconds—which is a marathon!—the fruits of tachiai cease to be a factor.

Moreover, there are some wrestlers, regardless of the above odds, who build successful makuuchi careers as Jumpers. Among current sumo's most intimidating Jumpers are yokozuna Hokutoumi, ozeki Konishiki, and Terao—who is slashingly quick and wildly inconsistent. When matched against a great Jumper, the other wrestler is often compelled to become a Jumper himself. This means he's trying to outjump the master, which increases the advantage for the more experienced Jumper.

The success of several very highly ranked Jumpers also demonstrates the effectiveness of a really great jump. In any contact sport, when you catch the other guy totally flatfooted, you are almost unbeatable. One of the matches in my statistical sample was a classic all-Jumper showdown between Hokutoumi and Terao. Terao blitzed Hokutoumi by—literally—stealing tachiai. Terao was up and in Hokutoumi's face while Hokutoumi was still getting up from his squat. Terao cheated, yes, but the ref didn't call it. On the same day in the same tournament, but with a different ref, Owakamatsu pulled a similar heist on Tamaryu. Tamaryu was beaten so badly that he thought Owakamatsu had false-started and he didn't even fight back.

So, y'see, once in a blue moon, a Jumper can steal a match. Terao might be the best tachiai thief in sumo history. Receivers, on the other hand (like Alan Ladd and the Lone Ranger), never steal. They rely instead, and wisely, on Bohr's Constant—which means that you don't mess with the percentages. Receivers, over the long haul, still have the edge.

There's a good reason for this, and its embodiment is, again, in the best rikishi of this generation, Chiyonofuji. Chiyo was a Receiver, one of the greats. Comparisons to Don Hutson, Jerry Rice, Johnny Bench. When he jumped—and he did sometimes—Chiyonofuji broke form. He abandoned the patience and precision that placed him in a class by himself. Chiyonofuji, as a Jumper, was merely average, and very beatable.

But when he waited . . .

Chiyonofuji read his opponent as the other guy was just rising from his squat. Chiyo met the charge with his right shoulder low and his right arm stiff against his chest. The left hand would dart at the other wrestler's belt. If the left missed the belt, Chiyo was unruffled, because his position was solid. The right shoulder was still low, the left hand still poised for attack. At this point, who got the jump on who is irrelevant, because the wrestlers are erect and active, facing each other in mid-dohyo. Chiyonofuji, because he was always the better wrestler, was under control. I watched him bounce off an opponent as many as five times, in that unique crouch, before finally getting his grip and reeling in, tightening up and flattening the poor slob.

Receivers tend, like Chiyonofuji, to be superior wrestlers. All wrestling is, at bottom, a balance of move and countermove. It is the transformation of a good defensive posture into a strong offensive thrust. Jumping at tachiai can be a devastating offensive ploy, but unless it is immediately and decisively successful, it tends to leave the rikishi in a defensive position that is so weak that he must scramble to recover.

For instance, I remember a high school wrestler from Milwaukee named Hector Cruz. Hector had only one hand. The other was there, but it was shriveled, and essentially useless. Theoretically, every one of Cruz' opponents needed only to attack Cruz on the side of the crippled hand. Which they did—which, of course, is exactly what Cruz wanted them to do. Cruz had built his entire defensive posture around the protection of that huge, obvious physical weakness. All of his offensive moves, therefore, grew from that defensive preoccupation. If you attacked Hector's crippled hand, he was waiting for you. You were toast.

Hector Cruz (he was a Receiver because his body forced him to be) won the state championship that year because his opponents usually misjudged him at the start of the match—and went downhill from there.

"Fast Is Good, Heavy Is Better"

In sumo—each match little more than six seconds—the start is even more critical. In sumo, the start is almost always the finish. The quality of tachiai determines victory or defeat at least two-thirds of the time (probably more). If nothing else, my statistics emphasize the intuitive physics of Bohr's Constant. Countermoves prevail over moves just about 60 percent of the time.

Disregarding statistics, the texture of a sumo match expresses this tendency even more clearly. You can spot the underdog because he's the one who looks nervous. The favorite exudes confidence, even arrogance. While the underdog coils for a lightning attack, his legs bunching, his shoulders leaning across the white line, the favored rikishi settles comfortably into a vigilant crouch. His tension is in his eyes—watching, studying, anticipating. Since he has studied his opponent's tendencies and limitations, he usually gets the attack he expects. There's no reason to hurry. Indeed, if he did hurry, he'd be wasting the skill and experience that gives him—even before tachiai—the upper hand. For the rikishi who brings to the match a touch of athletic genius, six seconds is an eternity.

So, "Go ahead," his eyes say. "Make my day."

Former rikishi Shinko amends this recipe for a good tachiai. "Fast is all right, but heavy is better," said Shinko. A very fast charge at tachiai tends to extend the upper part of the rikishi's body out in front of him. Since rikishi—blessed as they are with bellies bigger than beer kegs—tend to be top-heavy, this lightning thrust can simply become a fatal imbalance, especially when the other rikishi doesn't cooperate. If he doesn't grab you and hold you up, you can be facedown in the dirt in nine-tenths of a second. Many matches end this way.

I thought it a clever tactic for a lighter rikishi to move laterally at tachiai against bigger opponents. But Shinko said no, for the same reason: balance. Even if a rikishi is heavily outweighed, "He has to go straight in—head-to-head," said Shinko.

There's a measure of machismo in this outlook, but it also makes sense as strategy. In boxing, a basic coaching tenet is "stick and move." The word order is instructive. In sumo—even more than in boxing— you have to make solid contact. Smash that sucker, stop him in his tracks, and then—if you must—start dancing. Stick again, move again. Mobility without contact is simply a postponement of the inevitable.

Ideally, said Shinko, the rikishi comes in low and quick, with his head up. His weight is centered on his hips and thighs. His feet are spread and moving forward in short, powerful steps. This is a "heavy" tachiai.

As indicated, however, by the success of several reckless Jumpers, there are rikishi who do just fine with a tachiai that's all light and goofy. Athletic skill, body type, emotional stability, the identity of the opponent—all these things alter a rikishi's style of tachiai, and serve, now and then, to upset the percentages. No rikishi clings invariably to a single approach. He couldn't survive if he were so predictable. But in any given match, the two rikishi fall into one of five categories.

The Five Styles of Tachiai
Dividing them into groups, you've got your hook-

ers, your bulldozers, your boxers, your stranglers and your matadors.

The HOOKER is the classic sumo wrestler. He extends his strong hand (Chiyonofuji's dangerous left) as he bursts from his squat, reaching out to hook his opponent's mawashi with his fingers. Rikishi fall short of many other athletes in areas like abdominal muscle-tone, but they have perhaps the strongest hands in the sports world—because of all the clawing and clinging necessary for the perfect, unbreakable belt-grip.

A hooker who, on the first grab from tachiai, gets his grip, is most of the way to winning the match.

The BULLDOZER is a rikishi who depends on exceptional body mass and a powerful launch. He puts his head down, rather than up, fires forward (often off-balance), plants his paws in the other guy's gut, then rips and flails like a crazed Cape buffalo tipping over a tourist bus. When all this body English meshes, the bulldozer is simply unstoppable and the only defense is to get the hell out of his way. If you can. Bulldozers are pretty quick. Hesitate, and you're on your heels until you're off the dohyo.

My favorite bulldozer ever was a Samoan named Nankairyu, who had shoulders like an ox and legs like a diesel locomotive. When he launched his full charge and hit an opponent head-on, they both ended up in the fifth row, and it was up to the ring judges to decide who landed first. Unfortunately, Nankairyu was predictable. Other rikishi regularly anticipated his lunatic rush and countered it with increasing effectiveness. Unable to master any other techniques, Nankairyu hung up his cup and went back to Samoa—breaking my heart but probably pleasing his mom. (Sumo nerds also note that Nankairyu had an array of poignant personal problems, but who cares? This is a sumo jock, not Julien Sorel.)

BOXERS explode from tachiai with two methods of attack, called *tsuppari* and *hataki*. Both can be translated, simply, as "hitting," or open-handed boxing. They batter the other rikishi's chest, shoulders, head and face with a furious flurry of blows, some of them violent enough to draw blood and all of them richly entertaining. Boxers force their opponents to box back. Tsuppari/hataki attacks serve two possible results. The preferred result is that the boxing assault so overwhelms the victim that he staggers backward across the tawara. If that doesn't work, the boxer strives to knock his opponent momentarily off balance, so that he can grab something—head, arm, shoulder, belt, nostril—that will give the boxer leverage.

Tsuppari and hataki are savage, simple, wonderful to watch and—when they work—withering. The problem is that boxing robs both rikishi equally of their balance. The attacker is just as likely as the receiver to find himself cartwheeling off the dohyo and landing in somebody's obento. Nevertheless, because boxing is a mainstay for lightweight underdogs to fend off Hippos, bulldozers and other pituitary mutants, it will remain forever a fundamental element of sumo.

A STRANGLER is a boxer who doesn't bother to hit the other guy. He rises from his squat, extends one hand, clamps it on the other guy's throat, and pushes the poor bastard's larynx into the bleachers. The unfailing characteristics of stranglers are (a) real good upper body strength, and (b) a grip like a vise. Hokutoumi, for instance, could give a few pointers to Albert DeSalvo. He is one of few rikishi who can virtually lead an opponent off the dohyo by his throat.

The disadvantage to this stranglehold (called *nodowa*) is that, with a powerful swipe, an opponent can break the grip and simultaneously tip the strangler off-balance. If a receiver can seize that instant of imbalance, the strangler becomes easy pickings.

Finally, everybody in sumo at one time or another plays MATADOR. All you have to do is pretend you're about to smash into the other guy with all your might. Then, instead, you jump aside, let the other guy go flying by, and watch him crash and burn on the sand. Maybe, just for good measure, you give him a little shove, a little whack upside the head as he goes by. The only thing missing in this scene is a red cape.

The matador move works, at times, against any unwary rikishi, but it's especially effective (and funny) against chronic bulldozers. Nankairyu gave up sumo mainly because everyone started playing matador against him. In some matches, he looked like a Keystone Kop in a Hal Roach comedy— charging pellmell to smash open a door only to see it swing open at the last second.

The matador move, however, is used sparingly— for two reasons. The first is that the Sumo Association tends to frown on matadors. According to the prevailing mythology, the true rikishi is a macho guy who smashes headlong into obstacles and scrambles his brains with reckless valor. The matador move is too clever and evasive—you can win without even touching the other guy—to enjoy favor among sumo's scramblebrained traditionalists.

The other reason not to overdo the matador maneuver is that it can backfire against a good Receiver. A seasoned Receiver can twist suddenly into a matador while he's still perched perilously on his elusive tippy-toes and, hence, is completely vulnerable. When this—commonly known as the Old Switcheroo—happens, there is no defense. For instance, I never saw Chiyonofuji, the Nureyev of the Old Switcheroo, beaten by a matador. The rest of the guys gave up even trying it against him.

Sumo's guardians frown on the matador defense for the same reason they fume at Konishiki's staredowns. It's gamesmanship. The Sumo Association prefers the comforting fiction that sumo is unsoiled by guile, deceit and base trickery. However, as we see, the entire prelude to the match is electric with gamesmanship—and much more amusing because of it.

To Live and Die at Tachiai

Tachiai is the climax of the battle of wits. Even though, logically, the advantage lies with those who react rather than with those who leap, there is a deepseated temptation to fool the ref, sneak a huge jump and steal a cheap victory in the grueling midst of a the fifteen-day tournament. That's why the Sumotori Rag enjoys such infinite variety, and why all the pose-striking unfolds with such mirthless gravity. That's why rikishi maneuver until the very last seconds before the charge.

That's why sumo's final squat, just before tachiai,

is a great moment in sports. The wrestlers creak into position, tug at their belts, paw the dust, stare blankly at the ground, arrange delicately the useless fringe *(sagari)* that hangs from the front of their mawashi, and watch each other intently as one hand, then the other, stretches down, touches the sand and gradually, exquisitely, precipitates the crash.

Some rikishi add features to this drama. Mitoizumi (the Asshole), for instance, habitually calls off the squat, insisting that he's not ready—forcing the ref to relax his goombai and start the squat over. Recently, I noticed a few of Mitoizumi's opponents deliberately false-starting, barging into him before he could pull his "I'm not ready" routine.

Touché!

False starts are a common device, and they're often intentional—as intimidation or as a tension release. When they happen, the ring judges look distressed. If one basho features too many false starts, Futagoyama punishes all the rikishi like schoolboys by convening an all-day tachiai seminar. He invariably complains that this new generation of rikishi can't do tachiai like they did in the old days. This is nonsense, but it injects into the gamesmanship of tachiai an odor of the forbidden that enhances its enjoyment.

When a rikishi false-starts accidentally, though, it often tips the balance of gamesmanship hopelessly against him. The one advantage that the two opponents share—as they mirror each other through the Sumotori Rag and the last squat—is mystery. They don't know, for sure, what the other guy is gonna do. This mystery is especially deep among old wrestlers, who get cagier as their talent collapses into sawdust and cholesterol.

A false start can shatter the mystery—reveal a rikishi's plan before he can even execute it. If his strategy is exposed in a false start, he has perhaps five seconds to make a new plan and apply to it the full force of his will—which is almost impossible (especially considering the dim intellect of your average jock).

Even if a rikishi has preserved the mystery of his strategy, he is exposed at the very instant of tachiai. Whatever he is going to do is done, in the blink of an eye. All of sumo's strategy is concentrated in that split second. There are a thousand moves and countermoves in sumo—as there are in every other wrestling sport. But the difference is that in sumo, every subsequent action lives or dies at tachiai. If Move No. 1 fails, you may never get to Move No. 2.

Stonewall and Jack Wilson—and Nankairyu, the Samoan madman—ended up learning the hard way the first principle of gunslinging, and sumo:

If you fumble the draw, ain't nobody shifty enough to duck the bullet.

THE FISTFIGHT

at the Malemute Saloon and Other Japanese Cultural Treasures

Now, I wouldn't want to suggest that, after tachiai, the rest of the sumo match is just a matter of mopping up—though this seems to be true in many cases. Once a rikishi has gained an advantage at tachiai—which is often tenuous—it is his to squander, and it is his opponent's to overcome. Herein, then, lies the drama of sumo, the heart of the matter.

The fight is the thing.

And here is sumo's heartwarming simplicity—because all a fan has to know is that one guy is trying to push the other guy into the dirt or off the dancefloor. Touch the ground with anything but your feet, set one little piggie over the straw ridge, and you lose. Time to go.

Perhaps more important, however, to all you tourists and culture vultures out there, is that those sweaty, grunting, thunderous few seconds between tachiai and the decision contain sumo's visual splendor and disturbing (or—if you're inclined that way—alluring) sensuality. Here is sumo's great jiggling mass of flesh, the almost sexual sprawl of naked men—bobbling breasts; moist, protuberant lips; pudgy hands grasping, groping, feeling, seeking purchase on the sweat-slicked body of another; pulsating buttocks; neon codpieces; thighs like Butterfly McQueen . . .

In a word: Culture!

This is the moment in sumo that drives observers—from the novice to the jaded commentator—to dizzy heights of socio-anthropological insight and raptures of overstatement. It's hard to keep your cool while watching Onokuni jump on top of Kyokudozan and squish him like a cockroach beneath a souvenir pillow-map of Mount Fuji. The verbal crapola that emerges in the heat of a day's sumo, especially after a few rousing matches, is almost unparalleled in sports, and it tends to distort the fan's perception of sumo as fun and games.

The Expert

For instance, during a recent broadcast, NHK's guest commentator was an American I'll mercifully refer to as Fred. He was an amiable-looking gaijin whose foremost physical feature was—as I recall—a gray fright wig. Fred's apparent qualifications for commenting authoritatively on sumo's intricacies stemmed from his hobby as a sumo photographer— which even got him a gig as illustrator for a coffee-table book that was hurriedly published for an emerging group of overseas sumo enthusiasts. Besides his avocation as a sumo photographer, Fred is, if I understood his introduction, teaching something at some Japanese university—which unfortunately tells us very little about his ability in that or any other academic discipline. Like many gaijin in Japan, Fred's genuine talents are difficult to judge because he has been pressed into service by his eager Japanese hosts to spout expertise in a dazzling variety of fields, not because he is a genius but because he savvies the local lingo.

I manfully maintained an open mind about Fred's sumo wherewithal until he exposed himself with the following statement:

"You can't understand Japanese culture unless you understand sumo."

This breathtaking simplification— a common feat among gaijin spokesmen in Japan—inevitably won murmurs of xenophobic approval from the NHK flacks who man the mikes. It served, after all, to reinforce the official sumo propaganda package. The NHK boys urged Fred on to further banalities while I pondered variations on this always popular "You can't understand . . . unless . . . " motif. The one that struck the truest note to me was one that has occurred to me often as I watched the matches on NHK: "You can't really understand sumo (ergo, Japanese culture) unless you understand basketball."

A wild conjecture! Gerry Tarkanian a repository of Oriental mystery?

It can't be true, but there's a point. Anyone versed in the fundamentals of many sports will quickly grasp the mind and method that govern rikishi during the apparently frantic burst of clutching and pounding that follows tachiai. In that perception, the observant fan will grasp that this classic, visceral clash contains nothing especially mysterious. In the central moment of the sumo experience, there is, indeed, more of man-to-man coverage than social mores. Here—as any observer of NBA paint combat, or NFL trench warfare, knows—a full appreciation of what's happening within these desperate seconds comes best from watching the monsters' hands and feet.

Hands, Feet, and Angles

Sumo is a wrestling sport, which means that—most of the time—skill, balance and intellect will beat sheer size and brute force. To see how this happens, how Akinoshima—a veritable nymph at 1.76 m (5'9") and 135 kg (297 pounds)—can compile a 9–2 record versus Konishiki—1.87 m (6'2") and 233 kg (513 pounds)—the educated fan tears his eyes away from those amber waves of flab and looks for Akinoshima's hands.

Chances are those meathooks are frantically hammering at Konishiki's arms. And Konishiki's hands are pumping in awesome thrusts toward Akinoshima's throat, seeking the stranglehold that Konishiki can use to simply march the smaller man off the dohyo. Unless Konishiki can get the grip he wants, his enormous size is a dangerous burden, teetering on hips and knees which—regardless of how awesome they look—are too small to move him safely in the feints and circles that Akinoshima prefers. Akinoshima slaps, claws and yanks at Konishiki's immense arms, battling to force the giant, just once, to sway unsteadily. Then, Konishiki must relent in his assault and regain his balance, which permits Akinoshima to seize the offense, snapping and punching at Konishiki like a magpie harassing a crow.

HANDS, in sumo, dictate offense.

Chiyonofuji, for instance, never lost when he reached in, through a desperate opponent's guard, and hooked a solid belt grip. He was equally dangerous with (a) his left arm on the belt over the other guy's arm (*hidari-uwate*, for you would-be nerds), or (b) his right arm on the belt inside the other guy's arm *(migi-yotsu)*. He would attack either side with equal tenacity and sink that grip deeper and deeper as his opponent struggled against it. And then he'd drag his victim down.

As he aged, Chiyonofuji was beaten when he fell into a predictable pattern of going repeatedly for one side. He was also vulnerable when the other guy worked like mad to keep Chiyo's hands off his mawashi. Without his grip, Chiyonofuji was a small man fighting a big guy, and things tend to even out.

The point, above all, is that once you'd watched Chiyo through a dozen matches, you concentrated on his hands, on his opponent's hands, because you knew that the whole match lay in where they each got—or didn't get—a grip.

After hands comes, no, not feet—we'll get to that— the mawashi, the belt. It is an irony of sumo that its practitioners are regarded as the nakedest (not counting those naughty ancient Greeks; and I'm leaving out lady Jell-O wrestlers, too, OK?) of all grapplers. The tank-top, short-legged, crotch-grabbing jumpsuit worn by amateur wrestlers is intended to simulate nudity, but covers all the erogenous zones, as do the lollipop panties favored by professional wrestlers. Sumo wrestlers look nakeder because their cheeks are out there for all the women of Japan to admire and compare.

However, in a practical sense, the sumo wrestler is less naked than all his fellow grapplers. The key to all sumo technique lies in the mawashi, which is wrapped so many times around the rikishi's waist (I'm not sure how many times around, but Doreen knows, and she insists that Lora doesn't) that it sticks out. You can use the belt for leverage. The presence of the mawashi, around each rikishi's ample middle, makes sumo the only wrestling sport in which your opponent is not functionally nude; the only wrestling sport in which you have something other than a body part to grab a hold of.

The MAWASHI is the attacker's goal and the defender's weakness. Because the mawashi naturally evolved, many moons ago, as a magnet for the sumo wrestler's strength and imagination, it turned sumo inevitably into an above-the-waist wrestling sport. There is no ban on leg-hold in sumo, but leg-holds are almost nonexistent. Some wrestlers attempt leg-holds in desperation, but usually—just as quickly— let go, as though they'd just stuck a hand into something dead and smelly. Leg-holds carry a stigma of cowardliness. They suggest that, jeez, if you gotta trip the other guy to win, maybe you should go into another line of work, like nursing, or hairdressing.

This explains, logically, why the better rikishi are deft in belt technique, and why—often apparently in

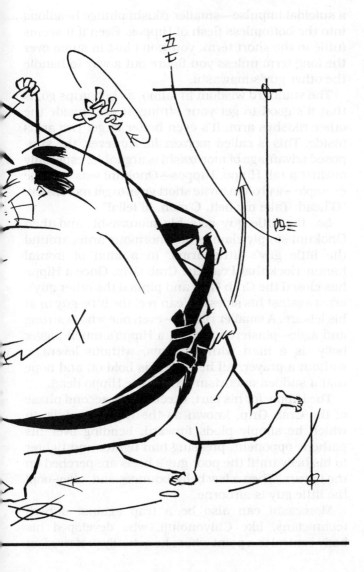

a suicidal impulse—smaller rikishi plunge headlong into the bottomless flesh of Hippos. Even if it seems futile in the short term, you won't last in sumo over the long term unless you figure out a way to handle the other guy's mawashi.

The standard wisdom in sumo, as belt grips go, is that it's good to get your strongest arm inside the other rikishi's arm. It's even better to get two arms inside. This is called *morozashi*. However, the supposed advantage of morozashi is arguable, especially against a tall Hippo. Hippos—Onokuni was a prime example—will often invite short guys to get morozashi. "G'head. Take my belt. C'mon, lil fella!"

So, the little guy gets his morozashi, and then Onokuni simply clamps his enormous arms around the little guy's little arms, in a kind of frontal hammerlock that I call the Crab Grip. Once a Hippo has closed the Crab Grip and pinned the other guy's arms against his sides, he can reel the little guy in at his leisure. A smaller rikishi—even one who is strong and agile—plastered against a Hippo's much bigger belly, is a man without arms, without leverage, without a prayer. All he can do is hold on and hope that a sudden aneurism strikes the Hippo dead.

The Hippo, for his part, executes the second phase of the Crab Grip, known as the Hippo Waddle, in which he simply plods forward, bending over his pathetic opponent, pressing him tighter and tighter to his belly until the poor guy's heels are perched on the tawara. Then a few belly-bounces and, alley-oop! the little guy is airborne.

Morozashi can also be a trap against superb technicians, like Chiyonofuji, who developed his body control to a point where he actually preferred an outside grip, because it afforded him superior leverage. In many matches, Chiyonofuji conceded morozashi without giving an inch.

FEET, in sumo, dictate defense.

As all that hand jive unfolds, the rikishi who forgets to use his footwork to his advantage is like a basketball player with footprints on his chest. Good rikishi will always keep their weight on the balls of their feet, evenly distributed in a broad stance—the classic defensive pose in basketball. When rikishi lock into the familiar stalemate position, heads on each other's shoulders, hands on each other's mawashi, they extend their legs back as far as possible from the other rikishi, for balance. One foot is slightly forward of the other, thus balancing the rikishi's forward and backward, as well as lateral, movement.

The best example for the importance of footwork in sumo is probably Terao, who has built a delightfully inconsistent record around his superb sense of natural balance—and his Mr. Hyde tendency to completely ignore it at times. Terao's tachiai resembles an active firehose without a fireman attached. He comes in, spraying punches in all directions, intent on knocking his usually larger opponent off balance while concealed in a cloud of dust. When he concentrates on keeping his stance wide throughout this blitz, he virtually doubles his size, and sends his disoriented opponent reeling off the dohyo—or diving for a spot where Terao was just a second ago. Thump.

On the other hand, Terao loses his concentration as regularly as Xaviera Hollander loses her virtue. He has a habit of getting his legs together, or even

THE FISTFIGHT • **150**

crossing them as he pursues—or flees—his opponent. When that happens, you can usually count to about three before Terao lands—upside down—somewhere in the fifth row. Terao's cartwheels into the crowd are one of sumo's highlights.

And they are a classic illustration of why a solid defensive position is fundamental to sumo, or basketball.

ANGLES, in sumo, suggest the advantage. But not always.

Any time a rikishi can turn his opponent, he has leverage. He is moving straight ahead against the opponent, while the opponent is applying his strength sideways, inefficiently. The other guy's in trouble.

When two rikishi have their shoulders parallel, and on the same vertical plane, they're stalemated, feeling for a better grip, working for position, thinking. If one of them changes the plane of that parallel, so that his shoulders are above—or below—the opponent's shoulders, an advantage emerges again. However, the advantage in this situation—when the rikishi remain face-to-face but not shoulder-to-shoulder—isn't determined by angles. Then the difference goes back to the relative position of hands and feet.

Here's how angles play a decisive role. In the Nagoya Basho, 1990, Takamisugi (Butterball, 145 kg) was wrestling Kyokudozan (Jock, 101 kg). Both of them knew that, face-to-face, Takamisugi has the edge, because he's heavier, and he might be able to simply bulldoze the stronger but smaller rikishi off the dohyo. Kyokudozan's strategy, when he wrestles, always has to counter this threat, so he tries to plant himself at an angle to his opponent's body.

Takamisugi, predictably, fired out powerfully at tachiai and moved Kyokudozan back, almost to the tawara. Kyokudozan bounced off Takamisugi and sidestepped, momentarily getting an angle. But Takamisugi, an old warhorse who knows the danger of pushing an advantage too hard too fast, suspended his charge and turned into Kyokudozan. Splat. Face-to-face. Stalemate. They nuzzled each other's necks for a moment, clung to each other's mawashi. They waited. Loosing his grip on the left, Kyokudozan—using his speed advantage—jumped to the right, pulling hard on his right-hand grip to unbalance Takamisugi and upend him with an arm-throw. It didn't quite work. Takamisugi is a mite too heavy to just toss around like a beach chair, and he's also pretty quick for a whale. But Kyokudozan's move was still much better than Takamisugi's response, because he was able to hold a position with his shoulders at a 45-degree angle to Takamisugi's. He had him. Takamisugi twisted, trying to regain the stalemate and backpedaled to give himself room. But as he did so, his feet closed, his grip lost its conviction. Kyokudozan pressed the advantage, driving into Takamisugi's shoulder—all the way off the dohyo.

Hands, feet and angles.

While this was all going on, there was a lot of noise. Screaming, to be exact. Not from the crowd. It's from the referee.

The Guy in the Pajamas

It always happens. By a rather felicitous tradition,

sumo has the most useless referees in all of sport. They dress really pretty, and sumo nerds wallow in explanations of the ritual significance of all the doo-dads and thingummies referees carry with them. And they carry a lot of thingummies. Kid Sheleen in full regalia, by comparison, was almost naked. Every referee, for instance, has his silk pajamas, of course, and a hat that makes him look like a bellhop balancing a flat-iron on his head, *tabi* (socks) and *zori* (sandals) on his feet, plus his goombai and a long silk rope he trips over during matches—and all these come in colors that tell you his rank, his family, his blood type, the year he first got laid—all kinds of good stuff! None of this, of course, means a thing.

OK, it means something. It's every bit as important as the color of the uniforms the umpires wore in the Federal League in 1914.

In any case, sumo referees have a lot of work just keeping their ensemble in order and their silk rope out from underfoot. So their workload during the match is pretty light. Mostly, they scream—in a nasal squeal that evokes the pork queue in a Chicago slaughterhouse. The sense of their screaming is distinctly unhelpful. Mainly, they shout, "Nokotta, nokotta, nokotta, nokotta, nokotta," etc. This means, "You're still in, you're still in, you're still in, you're still in, you're still in," etc. If the match lasts more than ten seconds, the ref intercedes on behalf of all the impatient fans out there in TV-Land who want to take another sip of their beer, and he screams, "Yoi, hakkeyoi!" ("Hey, move it!") Just the sort of thing you want to hear from an 85-pound septuagenarian geek while you're trying to move the Son of the Blob without benefit of a forklift.

Rarely, a referee leaps into the breach for a spasm of crisis management, largely because the world of sumo eschews the use of modern fastening technology—zippers, velcro, etc. Rikishi still get their mawashi tied in the back. In the heat of a match, a knot occasionally comes undone—at which the referee halts the hulks in mid-tussle, tells them to freeze in position, and then secures the troublesome knot. Considering the size difference between rikishi and ref, this touching scene tends to resemble an ant gift-wrapping a June bug.

It might happen, but in several years of sumo devotion, I've never seen a referee "call" a violation, personal foul or illegal hold on a rikishi. If a ref ever tried such a thing, it would prompt a big meeting in the middle of the dohyo, at which the five judges would talk, the referee would speak only when spoken to, and the five judges would then nod and solemnly return to their places, after which the head judge—who has more Sumo Association power in his little finger than any referee has stuffed under his entire nightgown—would gravely announce that the poor dumb ref is full of shit, sorry, folks, next match! And the referee's career would be over.

The Finish

This, then, is the essence of sumo for the eagle-eyed fan.

Hands.

Feet.

Little guys fighting for an angle.

Big guys hugging and waddling.

And pesky, impotent referees.

There's one other thing—the end of the match, the

winning move. Now, clearly, the winner does not execute his coup de grace without properly setting it up, with a good tachiai, deft hands and solid footwork. But most sumo nerds, in discussing what happened in any given match, cut right to the chase—which is the naming of the victorious move. This is not because they cherish brevity. They just like to toss around polysyllabic Japanese terms that most fans can't remember.

They like this part 'cause it's culture!

According to the experts, there are dozens of techniques that determine victory in a sumo match. My favorite expert, for instance, insists that there are 4,667 if you include *goombai taberu* (a rare technique that involves eating the referee's fan). The importance is that each "technique" is difficult to pronounce and is distinctly anticlimactic. I mean, after every middle-aged housewife in the audience has stood up, raised her fist and shouted, "Whoa! All right! In yo' face, fatso!" the solemn announcement that Terao employed *oshidashi* to secure the victory is depressingly tame.

Who cares? This is 'rasslin', not art history class. Shove 'im again!

Seriously, though, there is enlightenment to be gained from the rudiments of Sumo Climax Nomenclature (SCN). And even if there isn't, it's something you can't avoid if you watch the sumo matches regularly. Once a match is over, the scramble to name the move dominates the NHK broadcast. As soon as one guy wins, someone (I suspect it's the head judge) decides which technique was used. This decision is relayed to NHK, announced by the play-by-play announcer and flashed on the TV screen. The public adddress announcer tells the crowd. If it all sounds like gibberish, don't worry. The nice thing about SCN is that you, the fan, have a lot of people to take care of it for you. The Sumo Association, the regiment of sumo nerds, and the guys at NHK are all on duty, telling you incessantly who used what technique to whup whom.

Nevertheless, discerning a few key phrases from the TV announcer will help keep you on top of the action. Here they are.

1) SOMEBODY NO KACHI. "Kachi" means "win." When you're not sure who landed outside the ring first in a match between Jingaku and Kotonishiki, "Kotonishiki no kachi," tells you that Jingaku bit the dust.

There is also a handy visual aid if the TV camera catches it. The referee's proudest task is to point his goombai in the direction from which the winner entered the ring. The ref can be overruled by the ring judges occasionally, but most times, the goombai denotes the winner. Nice job, ref. Go to your room.

2) YORIKIRI. This is the commonest and most dignified way to win a sumo match, otherwise known as "the missionary position." It's also usually the dullest. When you hear "yorikiri," it means the winner was face-to-face with the loser, hugging him desperately and straining to push him backward across the tawara, often grinding his codpiece into his opponent's groin. Most rikishi are trained to fight for a two-hand belt-grip and taught that yorikiri is the manliest form of victory, requiring the maximum of strength, flab and technical virtuosity. I suspect that it's regarded with such esteem because it's easy

to teach to dumb jocks. Whether you call it a bear hug, the missionary position or yorikiri, it has the charm of brute instinct.

"Yorikiri" is usually the technique announced when two incompetent rikishi bungle through a chaotic brawl and collapse on top of each other. In the absence of even a vestige of technique, the usual Sumo Association policy is to put the best possible face on the mess: they invoke the missionary position and hope NHK loses the videotape.

The Hippo Waddle, by the way, is the dullest form of yorikiri.

3) SOMETHING-DASHI. There are a host of "-dashi" moves, but most mean that the winner shoved the loser off the dohyo, usually hard, usually all over the fans in the front row—who always giggle. *Oshidashi* is the commonest -dashi, and it is bread and butter for boxers and bulldozers. Stranglers like it, too.

Most -dashi are violent and unsophisticated, but *tsuridashi* is a notable exception. It is the piece de resistance of sumo's strongest and most athletic rikishi. It requires that the winner secure a vise-like two-handed belt grip and lift—literally carrying the other guy off the dohyo, as the victim kicks his legs helplessly. Tsuridashi, which puts dangerous pressure on the back, demands enormous strength and perfect timing. Chiyonofuji was a master of tsuridashi, but by mid-1990, he was surpassed in this technique by Kirishima, a new ozeki who changed his previously mediocre career through a diligent program of weight-training.

4) SOMETHING-TENAGE. All the -tenage (derived from *te*, "arm," and *nageru*, "to throw") are arm

throws, with the loser usually landing on his back inside the dohyo. Of all sumo moves, these tend to be the most sudden, graceful and athletic. A rikishi who works hard to get an "angle" on the other guy is usually working for -tenage. There are many such moves, and they often evolve spontaneously in a match after one or both of the rikishi have failed in other moves and find themselves tangled, side-by-side, trying to yank each other to the sand. Any -tenage is good entertainment. In the hands of Chiyonofuji, Asahifuji or one of the other good technicians, it's art.

Definitely more fun than yorikiri!

5) UTCHARI deserves special mention because it is sumo's most stunning move. In amateur wrestling, it would be called a "reversal." It usually occurs when a small, strong wrestler has been backed to the tawara by a bigger guy. He has a good belt grip, maybe even morozashi, but it isn't doing him much good because he's almost off the dohyo. Suddenly, he lifts and turns, executing what amounts to a twisting tsuridashi and throwing the big guy off the dohyo. Usually, the big guy drags him down too. But, in a well-executed utchari, the guy with his back to the wall lifts the other guy high enough and turns him far enough that he ends up landing on top of the loser. It is an extraordinary move—also hard on your back—that literally turns defeat to victory. Reversals only work because the winner has a better belt grip. Utchari is all the more dramatic because it usually requires a smaller rikishi to dead-lift a Hippo.

Two of the more astounding examples I've seen were Kyokudozan (101 kg, 222 pounds) reversing Kushimaumi (185 kg, 407 pounds)—without even locking his knees first, and Kirishima (127 kg, 279 pounds) reversing Onokuni (200 kg, 440 pounds).

6) HATAKI KOMI. The Matador (see Chapter 6).

7) MONO-II. In practical terms, this means, "Wait a minute," and it comes from any one of the five ring judges who might disagree with the referee's goombai in a very close match. Usually, mono ii are called when both wrestlers tumble off the dohyo together, or hit the dirt almost simultaneously. When a ring judge, who usually happens to be one of the ten biggest wheels in the Sumo Association, raises his hand for mono ii, all the judges gather on the dohyo with the referee, who is required to keep his trap shut unless asked a question.

The ring judges then consider a number of factors before deciding who really won. These include:

(a) Which wrestler actually touched down first. The ring judges are allowed to check video replays through an audio linkup with the TV truck. They don't look at the video tape, you understand. They hear about it.

(b) Which wrestler was making a more positive offensive move as the both of them crashed in a cloud of dust.

(c) Which wrestler comes from a more important sumobeya, and whether the Sumo Association wants to promote the interests of that stable.

The ring judges discuss only (a) and (b) above. The other, (c), is simply a tacit consideration that tends to outweigh (a) and (b).

Because of these conflicting considerations, the results of mono-ii are often surprising to the observant fan. Crews of ring judges rotate, and ring judges—even within the same crew—apply no consistent pattern to their decisions. In some cases when a decision seems impossibly close and mono ii strikes the observer as appropriate, the ring judges sit motionless, possibly asleep. This means that both rikishi are relatively unimportant and don't merit special attention from the muckymucks around the dohyo.

After mono ii, one of three results might be announced by the head judge—usually in an incomprehensible mumble over a microphone he keeps in his lap. Possibility No. 1 is that the judges endorse the ref's goombai. Possibility No. 2 is a decision reversal, which goes into the ref's record as a black mark. Possibility No. 3 is that nobody could tell who really won, so the two rikishi have to wrestle again.

Rematches after mono ii sometimes indicate real indecision (and real fairness) on the part of the ring judges. Sometimes, they are shrewd political moves that prevent the backlash that might come after a decision that offends a powerful sumobeya. In any case, the fan makes out, because you get to see an extra match. Chiyonofuji was usually great in rematches, because he got pissed off when he had to wrestle twice in one day.

Extra Terms

As I've already explained, the above terminology is more than the funloving fan needs to know. I add two additional terms that help me classify a match not by its conclusion but by the way it unfolds while the two guys are still up and slugging. These are:

1) "The Wild Boar Hunt," which describes what happens when a small, agile rikishi scurries around

the dohyo, poking and dodging in a desperate effort to unbalance a Hippo. Konishiki is involved in more than his share of Wild Boar Hunts, as the boar, and Terao is easily the most prolific and entertaining boar hunter.

The boar, by the way, usually wins anyway.

2) "Fistfight at the Malemute Saloon." Credit for the elevation of this wonderful variation really belongs to a young wrestler named Takatoriki, whose hataki (face-smacking) attacks display an almost unprecedented verve. Ideally, in a Fistfight at the Malemute Saloon, some chippy punk like Takatoriki will start trouble by really whacking the other guy hard, with one of those blows to the ear that make your head ring and your sinuses drain. This gets the other guy mad. As a rule, rikishi don't get mad, but Takatoriki is annoying enough to negate the rule. The little bastard makes you want to hit him back, real hard. So they do. Of course, he hits them back, even harder. Pretty soon, neither one is the least bit interested in grabbing a belt and winning the match. They just want to pound the crap out of each other. Meanwhile, the referee stands by helpless, just like the bartender at the Malemute. The two rikishi start bleeding from the mouth, nose, eyebrows, possibly even staining the ref's pajamas. The ring judges scowl disapprovingly. And the fans go wild. Eventually, Takatoriki, who knew what he was doing when he started the fistfight, puts a move on the other guy and wins.

Other rikishi, like Itai, Kotonishiki, and the Purple Prince, have been known to start Fistfights at the Malemute Saloon, but the sumo reincarnation of Dangerous Dan McGrew is unquestionably Takatoriki.

I hope the point I've made, in this description of sumo's action during the match, demonstrates that sumo—although it serves nicely as a View Master slide of Japanese culture—might better be seen as a game, a sport, a fistfight, a basketball clinic, or any one of a hundred other comparable pastimes.

Perhaps more important is the fact that you don't have to "understand" sumo—as Fred insisted while under the spell of a live microphone—to enjoy it, or even appreciate it. I loved basketball, for instance, before I even remotely understood it. I screamed and cheered and even got thrown out of the Tomah (Wisconsin) High School gym once when I was nine years old, for losing my cool in the bleachers. All this happened before I knew there was such a thing as a fundamental defensive position, before I knew the definition of goaltending, before I had ever heard of the pick-and-roll.

I just liked watching these great tall heroes from my own hometown battling the villains from enemy towns. I was like my son, Aaron, who saw his first sumo matches one day in Tokyo when he was fifteen. He didn't know *utchari* from *uchi-gake* (and neither do I), but he knew a good fight when he saw one. And he had fun, especially when Takatoriki started breaking another guy's eardrum, and when Konishiki crushed Kotofuji like a gumshoe landing on a cigar butt.

Fred and I—and Doreen and Andy and even Lora—all agree that the terminology and nuances create, in your average know-it-all, a proprietary interest in a sport. The little things fuel our addiction and breed our points of view. We argue with deep conviction and annoint our petty knowledge of esoterica by insisting that its importance is not in the sports arena but in the tabernacle of culture.

Priests, after all, get more respect than gallery gods.

But the monkey wrench in all this posturing is that sumo is still two fat guys in the dirt, slugging each other. And if they didn't do that, and if one of the fat guys didn't win and the other one didn't lose, there wouldn't be any "culture" to understand, at least not from sumo. We'd all end up in the museum, looking at pottery and playing with origami.

THE RIPSNORTER
in Nagoya

A sumo tournament (basho) is designed as a crescendo. If everything proceeds according to the Sumo Association's program, the importance of the matches, the tension, the excitement build steadily from Day 1 through Day 15—with the biggest thrills jammed into the very last match of the last day.

It doesn't always work out this way, partly because the Sumo Association has a knack for choreographing results and killing suspense. But with six basho a year, you get a great finale in sumo a lot more often than you get a nail-biting, down-to-the-wire Super Bowl or a high-scoring, run-and-gun World Cup final. Occasionally, there is an epic match, a perfect fight—what my old weatherbeaten Grandma would call a "ripsnorter." In Nagoya, July 22, 1990, Chiyonofuji and Asahifuji put on a ripsnorter.

As the match approached, my wife and I were torn. On the one hand, we both admired Chiyonofuji, for his athletic brilliance, his unconventional style, his class, and his gorgeous buns. On the other hand, we had a soft spot in our hearts for Asahifuji— because he never gets any respect. For three years, in our judgment, he had wrestled at yokozuna level without getting the appropriate rank. He kept beating people, but they wouldn't promote him from ozeki to yokozuna

So we wanted both of them to win.

The rest of Japan, excluding the village of Kizukuri in Aomori—Asahifuji's hometown—was more clearly in Chiyonofuji's corner. Even in Kizukuri, where about a hundred natives sat grimly on their haunches in the community center to watch the final match on NHK, the commitment to Asahifuji was weirdly restrained. Speaking to an NHK reporter on behalf of the town, the mayor of Kizukuri said Asahifuji was on the brink of being inducted into the village Hall of Fame. All he had to do was win this match and nail down his promotion. What if he lost, though?

The mayor hemmed, the mayor hawed. "Well, we'll see . . ."

The smaller the Hall of Fame, obviously, the tougher the entrance exam!

Besides the love of the nation, the bookies also favored Chiyonofuji. Everyone knew, after all, that Asahifuji was jinxed in Big Matches.

But things were different this time, weren't they? Asahifuji, for one thing, was leading this tournament. After fourteen days in Nagoya, he was 13–1, his only loss a screw-up against Ryogoku (Trashcan) on Day 3. Chiyonofuji, in second place at 12–2, had also blown his match with Trashcan. (Overall, Ryogoku had a mediocre basho, at 7–8, but he had two new segments for his private highlight film.)

After his loss to Trashcan, Asahifuji managed to regain his concentration, and wasn't seriously threatened again, even against his old nemeses like Tochinowaka, Konishiki, Akinoshima and Hokuto-umi.

Chiyonofuji's Ghosts

But Chiyonofuji lost again, on Day 8, to Kotonishiki, and stirred familiar concerns among both his friends and rivals. More than six months before, the only American sumo coach, Jesse Kuhaulua (who has three other names, by the way . . . rikishi name: Takamiyama; oyakata name: Azumazeki; Japanese name: Daigoro Watanabe) had bluntly said that Chiyonofuji was over the hill and he would hang up his codpiece in 1990. Chiyo quickly shut Jesse up by winning the 1990 New Year Basho in January. But the Wolf missed the title in March with a 10–5 record and lost in May at 13–2. When Kotonishiki overpowered Chiyo on Day 8 in Nagoya, even Chiyo's coach, Kokonoe, began to worry. Kokonoe was pessimistic before Chiyonofuji's Day 10 test against Akinoshima—a stubborn little defensive specialist everybody hates to wrestle. Akinoshima had actually spent one whole day as the unbeaten basho leader—before a resounding loss to Asahifuji. Regardless of his basho record, Akinoshima was always at his best against the best and he represented—with the possible exception of Konishiki—Chiyo's most fear-some opponent.

Against Chiyo this time, however, Akinoshima (talented but dumb) was out of his league. Chiyo came into the match with a plan and creamed the kid without breaking a sweat. "He rose like a phoenix," said Kokonoe. "I stopped worrying."

Yeah, but we didn't stop worrying. And neither, I suspect, did the Sumo Association. Chiyonofuji was sumo's official cover boy—on most editions of the official sumo program. When Japan Airlines produced a TV commercial featuring the 1990 Sumo Tour to Brazil, the guy the producers would put out front was a foregone conclusion. The Wolf. Everybody else in the commercial—including Futagoyama, the current head of the Sumo Association—brought up the rear.

Although it's easy to forget, Chiyonofuji had not always enjoyed such favor from the Establishment. When he decided to take some of his physical training outside the sacred dungeon of the sumobeya, to a fitness center where he lifted weights and sculpted his rippling mass of upper-body muscle, he violated a sumo taboo. Only when he became an idol of millions, the handsomest sumo star of the 20th Century, and the winningest rikishi of the '80s, did the Sumo Association declare no-hard-feelings and embrace Chiyonofuji as the symbol of all that is good and pure in the sport.

Chiyo was, indeed, a hard guy to hate. He was good looking, with a (relatively) small tummy, and that face—smooth, rugged, and kissable enough for a Noxzema commercial. His physique was, by any athletic standard, impressive. Naked, he could be

mistaken for an NFL linebacker, a heavyweight
contender or a large economy-size Cosmo centerfold.
His athleticism would make him a star in a dozen
other sports, and his charm results in thoughtful,
modest, humorous interviews. He was everybody's
favorite son.

Of course, this means that, coming into the final
match in Nagoya, he was under intense pressure. It
wasn't just a matter of fighting, from one loss down,
for the yusho (tournament championship) against
the hottest wrestler in sumo. Chiyonofuji was a
haunted man. The worst ghost was his age. He had
just turned 35, an age at which even the great rikishi
have given up hope for championships. He was also
haunted by his popularity. Because he was a kind of
Japanese national treasure, everyone expected him
to keep on winning forever, despite his age and the
odds and his size (he is among the smallest men in
sumo) and the strength of his younger, hungrier
opponents.

Finally, he had to cope with the dozens of ghosts of
sumo past, oldtimers who would not concede
Chiyonofuji's greatness unless he became the
winningest sumo wrestler of all time. In the March
Basho, Chiyo had become the first rikishi ever to win
a thousand matches, but he still needed two more
yusho to tie Taiho's 1956–71 record of 32 basho
championships. While once the march to the yusho
seemed easy for Chiyonofuji, it now demanded every
ounce of his strength and his will. The concentration
that used to make him invincible was now prone to
the occasional short circuit. A year before, that silly
loss to Trashcan would have been unthinkable.

The voices, the ghosts, kept telling Chiyonofuji,

from Day 1 through Day 15, that this basho, this crescendo might be his last chance.

Asahifuji's Jinx

The voices, however, were saying the same thing to Asahifuji. According to all of Japan's sumo pundits, this basho was Asahifuji's last chance for *tsunatori* (yokozuna promotion). Win or lose, he would be judged once more after the Nagoya basho. He'd won the Summer Basho in May with a 14–1 record, and he had 13 wins in this basho. The bigwigs had no choice but to give Asahifuji another chance—his seventh nomination. Six times before, he'd been rejected—for almost every reason under the rising sun, but mainly, they said, because he couldn't win the Big Match, the one at the very end against some fairhaired Kokonoe superstar (Chiyo or Hokutoumi). Asahifuji was the Minnesota Vikings, the Syracuse Orangemen, the Red Sox—always a bridesmaid, never a bride.

With this record of persistence and futility, Asahifuji looked like a natural for the role of Lovable Underdog. The crowds should have rooted for him affectionately; even the Sumo Association should have been quietly pulling for him.

Forget it. Hardly anybody really cared if Asahifuji made it or not. In his quest for yokozuna, he was all alone out there.

I think the reason is that Asahifuji, like Roger Maris and Kareem Abdul Jabbar, just isn't a very appealing guy. For one thing, he doesn't have any lips. And his head is too small for his body. These and other physical oddities meant that—no matter how hard he tried—Asahifuji just couldn't look, well . . . tough.

Consider, by comparison, Hokutoumi, Chiyonofuji's stablemate—also a yokozuna. You get the feeling, looking at Hokutoumi, that sumo was the only thing that steered him away from a life of crime. Hokutoumi looks, and fights, like the bully who chased you home from second grade, and then set fire to your cat. There was a memorable newsreel film, in 1990, of Hokutoumi visiting a little old Japanese lady in Brazil during the sumo goodwill tour. Even as Hokutoumi mugged for the cameras, one saw the pit bull glint in his eye and felt a nameless dread, that Hokutoumi might suddenly revert to his natural state, seize the old lady's head between his paws and crush it like a chocolate-covered cherry.

In the same newsreel, there were films of Asahifuji greeting little old Japanese ladies, and each one he met, he looked as though he was apologizing for not sending a Mother's Day card.

"I'm sorry, Grandma . . . I forgot, Grandma, I'm really sorry . . . Gosh, Grandma, it just slipped my mind . . ."

Pathetic.

Asahifuji is cursed with the face of a 297-pound weakling. The fickle public might have forgiven this flaw if Asahifuji had possessed some compensating virtue, like Chiyonofuji's beauty. If Asahifuji had been even slightly blessed in this respect and had developed a more than lukewarm public following, the Sumo Association might also have worked up a little enthusiasm for his promotion. But Asahifuji was one of the most ill-favored yokozuna candidates of modern times.

His six rejections for tsunatori were unprecedented. And a look at his record shows these rejections were not just unlucky, but unjust.

Over nine basho from January 1988 through mid-1989, Asahifuji had won more matches than either Chiyonofuji or Hokutoumi. His winning percentage (.825) was second to Chiyo's (.905), but ahead of Hokutoumi (.804). More important, he had a tougher schedule because while teammates Chiyonofuji and Hokutoumi never wrestled against one another, Asahifuji had to face both of them in every tournament. In the first three basho of 1989, Asahifuji's record against the Kokonoe duo was 5–2.

For this exceptional performance, Asahifuji was turned down three times in 1989 for promotion to yokozuna. The Sumo Association, of course, provided plenty of excuses.

For one thing, they insisted, it wouldn't be appropriate to award a promotion if Asahifuji had not won an outright championship. He'd lost two playoffs against Hokutoumi, but that wasn't good enough. The message here was that the Sumo Association didn't want another Futahaguro embarrassment.

Remember Futahaguro (alias Koji Kitao)?

In 1986, the Sumo Association had promoted Futahaguro, then a young, glamorous ozeki, to yokozuna, before he ever won a championship. Futahaguro's best finish was a tie for the yusho, after which he lost a wrestle-off (something Asahifuji does regularly). As it turned out, Futahaguro never did win a yusho. He settled down into the good life of being a pampered star, and in 1988 got into a fight

with his coach. Futahaguro was promptly kicked out
of sumo, banned for life and exiled to a clown's career
in Japanese professional wrestling, from which his
notoriety constantly reminded the Sumo Association
of its only yokozuna to ever "retire" without once
winning a title.

Also, said the Sumo Association in its yokozuna
refusals, they couldn't promote Asahifuji because he
didn't wrestle Chiyonofuji in one basho in early 1989
(because Chiyonofuji wasn't there). Two wins in two
tries wasn't convincing enough, especially since—
until 1989—Asahifuji's record against Chiyo was 2–
24.

Then, for five basho, from July, 1989 through
March, 1990, the issue of Asahifuji's promotion
became moot. He went into a decline that seemed to
seal his status permanently at ozeki. Part of this
regression stemmed, I think, from mental fatigue.
The pressure of maintaining so high a level of
performance for eighteen months, plus the repeated
disappointments, finally caught up to Asahifuji. His
body sagged, his mind cracked and his guts went
sour. In mid-1989, Asahifuji suffered a flareup of his
chronic illness, pancreatitis—an occupational haz-
ard caused by the rich, fat-laden diet that all rikishi
devour. Despite relentless pain, however, Asahifuji
kept wrestling, through records of 8–7, 9–6, 8–7, 9–6,
8–7.

To keep going, Asahifuji and his wife Junko
formulated a diet of mushy food that would sustain
Asahifuji's weight while soothing his delicate tummy.
Wherever he traveled, he took along special pots and
utensils for cooking this mush. By all rights,
however, Asahifuji should have been finished—

because he could not have the one thing he needed most: rest.

The sumo world has yet to discover the concept of sports medicine, or to discover the fact that "playing with pain"—if carried too far—can ruin, or even kill, athletes. Sumo embodies the conviction that Vince Lombardi immortalized when he said. "Nobody is hurt. Hurt is in the mind. If you can walk, you can run."

Or limp out onto the dohyo and slug it out against the Pudding that Ate Chicago! An injured or ailing rikishi is not expected to "grin and bear it." He is encouraged to "scowl and aggravate it," a fact that made Asahifuji's return to form in 1990 all the more surprising.

In May, 1990, Asahifuji won the Summer Basho. He was 14–1. He beat everyone except Chiyonofuji (13–2). Now, with two yusho, Asahifuji was up again for promotion. His rejection in May, however, was no surprise. The excuses were familiar. His previous basho (8–7) was mediocre, and—even though he won the May yusho—he didn't beat Chiyonofuji.

There was a new excuse, too. The Sumo Association stressed its reluctance to promote anyone to yokozuna unless they had won two—count 'em, two—yusho in a row. This was a tricky wrinkle, because it had been seventeen years since any rikishi had charged quite so triumphantly into the yokozuna ranks. According to the *Asahi Shimbun,* that was a guy named Kotozakura, who'd gone 9–6, 14–1 and 14–1, with two straight championships, in 1973. None of Asahifuji's contemporaries, not Onokuni, Hokutoumi, Chiyonofuji or the notorious Futahaguro, had won back-to-back yusho before their elevation.

Another complaint emerged from several highly placed detractors in the Sumo Association. It was often said that Asahifuji's sumo style was "weak." The explanation of this charge is that Asahifuji's strength always lay in his defensive skill. He absorbed his opponent's charge, positioned himself well, and usually initiated his winning move after an offensive foray by the opponent. Asahifuji won with reflexes, agility and cunning. This is hardly a description of "weak" sumo, but it was enough to saddle him with the charge that his game was not "complete." The same charge, of course, applied even more emphatically to Hokutoumi and Onokuni, whose offensive skills were resoundingly two-dimensional. Among Asahifuji's contemporaries in the upper ranks, only Chiyonofuji was a real virtuoso of offense. An objective ranking of "strong" sumo, made in spring, 1990, would have put Asahifuji solidly in second place.

Sumo is not an objective sport. The handwriting was on the wall in thick, red ink. The big boys were hardballing Asahifuji. But why?

The Sumo Association's objections went deeper than Asahifuji's unlovely face and "weak" style. A big drawback was that Asahifuji did not wrestle out of a powerful sumobeya. His oyakata, Oshima, is an excellent coach, admired by most in the sumo world. But Oshima is not a power broker in the Sumo Association. In the world's most incestuous sports organization, Asahifuji got no points for being well-connected.

Even worse, Asahifuji lost points with his uncoop-erative attitude toward *yaochozumo*, Japanese for "arranged matches"—in other words, "taking a dive."

In sumo, every rikishi—in order to create or repay debts—tanks a match from time to time. But Asahifuji was not an enthusiastic participant in this tradition. He might, for instance, have greased his promotion in 1990—regardless of his record—if he hadn't made Hokutoumi work so hard in those two 1989 wrestle-offs.

By playing it straight over the years, Asahifuji had made life complicated for his "betters," especially the boys from the Kokonoe stable (Hokutoumi and Chiyonofuji)—which, for most of the 1980s, was sumo's flagship, its glamor factory.

This, at bottom, was why the final match of the Nagoya Basho, 1990, was a ripsnorter in the making. It was a grudge match between two wrestlers, and two sumobeya, who didn't like each other and didn't make deals with each other, and didn't let the Sumo Association make deals for 'em. This meant—and all the smart fans knew it—that this match was the genuine article.

And you couldn't pick a favorite. Once, Chiyonifuji had dominated Asahifuji completely. But in the last eight basho, Chiyo's edge was only 5–3. Asahifuji was catching up.

Everyone knew that this match pitted the Establishment vs. the Party-Crasher. The Sumo Association didn't really want Asahifuji in the Club. If he was going to make it, he had to barge in, take on the Club champ, and then make sure he was the only one still on his feet when the dust settled.

In Nagoya, technically, Asahifuji had two cracks at the Champ—because he had a one-match lead. "I knew that if I lost," said Asahifuji, "I had another chance (in a wrestle-off)."

Think again, ferret-face!

The Sumo Association was watching Asahifuji for the slightest misstep. If he lost to Chiyonofuji and then won the wrestle-off, he was only 1–2 in two basho against the Sumo God, and 6–30 for his career.

Not good enough, chump.

At that moment, the clearest fact of life for Asahifuji (or for any aspiring rikishi) was that the price of glory in sumo was to beat—or suck up to— Chiyonofuji. All roads to promotion led, literally, through the Wolf.

The magic that radiated from that ripsnorter in Nagoya was that the fans knew Chiyonofuji had the Establishment on his side, and he didn't need them. He had defied the Club himself once, and he was a genius in his sport. He didn't need anybody's help to whip Asahifuji.

Meanwhile, Asahifuji finally had his body, his mind and his talent to the point where he was Chiyonofuji's equal. No one else could touch his record of 27–2 in the last two tournaments. He, too, was OK all by himself. He could beat the Champ.

Together, these were the two finest, most deter- mined, most desperate rikishi to face off for all the marbles in years.

The Match

I leaned toward the TV.

Chiyonofuji, after the last crouch, had indulged himself in a little staring and pose-striking with Asahifuji—unusual for him. Asahifuji's lipless mouth turned into a pencil line between his little nose and his little chin. He pounded his belt.

After a long (5 minutes, 30 seconds) Sumotori Rag,

they step out for tachiai. The head ref, Shonosuke Kimura (actually, all head refs are Shonosuke Kimura; this one's real name was Sokichi Kumagai), holds up his goombai and tells the boys to go when they feel the urge . . .

Chiyonofuji's urge comes first . . .

If anything typified Chiyonofuji's anxiety at growing older, it was the fact that in 1990, many times, he didn't wait at tachiai, to measure his opponent and react.

This time, Chiyo gets a huge jump. His left hand lunges and slaps Asahifuji's face while Asahifuji is still rising from his crouch . . .

But Asahifuji, whose eyes never waver from Chiyonofuji, gets the reward of waiting. His left hand, outside Chiyonofuji's right arm, finds a solid belt grip. His right hand sneaks inside Chiyo's dangerous left. As they meet, Chiyonofuji's feet are too far forward, literally under his chin and too close together. Asahifuji's feet are in balance, behind him and spread. His tachiai is "heavy," and—for a few precious seconds—Chiyonofuji is light . . .

Chiyo feels it. He stretches his right hand inside to Asahifuji's belt. But as he does, Asahifuji pulls hard with his left hand. This moves Asahifuji momentarily beside Chiyo, and Chiyonofuji then has to adjust, shifting his right hand to the middle of Asahifuji's belt, right under his navel. It's a deep belt grip, but hard to use . . .

Asahifuji attacks again, swings to the left, tightening his left hand. Chiyo counters, clutching Asahifuji's left arm as they spin together. Asahifuji broadens his stance, holds his balance. He coils his legs now, ready to drive into Chiyonofuji . . .

Chiyo senses the coming charge. He pushes back and tries to brace himself. But Asahifuji still has him turned, pressing Chiyo's right shoulder . . .

Chiyo now has to do something. Asahifuji is pushing him around, closing his grip and shrinking the dohyo . . .

Move, now!

Chiyo moves, reeling in Asahifuji with his right hand, suddenly jerking his 300-pound opponent like a Muppet.

As he pulls, Chiyonofuji staightens up, drawing his feet under him, stretching for Asahifuji's belt with his left . . .

Now the fans see what Chiyo is doing. Summoning his power. The sound they create is one of breath drawn hungrily into 10,000 throats . . .

Not yet, kids.

Asahifuji, whose agility is a match for Chiyonofuji and whose reactions are his mainstay, feels Chiyo pulling him tight, and he moves, too. He drives, twists left, grabbing Chiyonofuji's mawashi with his right hand inside. A moment of struggle, belly-to-belly, and they're stalemated . . .

"I pulled him into my body," said Chiyonofuji after the match. "That was a mistake."

But not a fatal mistake. It's just that Chiyo, outmaneuvered by Asahifuji, was now holding onto a mess. His right hand had slipped to the left. Asahifuji's mawashi climbed up his body as Chiyo pulled on it. Now Chiyo had a clumsy belt grip. Instead of holding Asahifuji by the waist, he was tugging at his chest.

Chiyo's left outside grip was also high, but a little tighter than his right hand. He had to keep that left grip; it was his strong side—now, his only anchor. Asahifuji, on the other hand, now had a left outside belt grip that was deep and dangerous.

Chiyo can't risk waiting. He makes the first of several powerful upper-body twists, pulling at Asahifuji's belt with his left hand while rocking to the right . . .

Asahifuji can't keep the right hand grip under Chiyo's violent pressure. He has to let go. He rocks onto one leg—his first moment off-balance. He clings with his left. He counters, gets his feet back. Asahifuji tightens his left, all the way behind Chiyonofuji's back. He lowers his shoulder into Chiyonofuji's chest . . .

Asahifuji drives. Chiyo strains to stop him. Chiyo backpedals, his feet shuffling toward the ridge . . .

Chiyo turns, another flash of power—Asahifuji powerless in Chiyonofuji's arms for one split second—escaping to the left . . .

This was the first critical moment, because Asahifuji's grip, his balance were good enough to beat almost any other human being. Against Chiyonofuji, Asahifuji gained, at most, 24 inches of space on the dohyo.

Chiyonofuji seizes the offense. A left arm throw, *uwatenage*, shakes Asahifuji but fails. Asahifuji reacts. He leans on Chiyo's right side. Chiyo retreats, feeling the sand under his feet, slipping . . .

He feels the ridge, plants his feet. The crowd murmurs, terrified, thrilled. Asahifuji hugs Chiyonofuji, adjusts that deep lefthand hold on Chiyo's mawashi. He's ready . . .

The quick kill! Yorikiri!

No!

He hurried too much. Asahifuji isn't set, and Chiyonofuji, somehow, feels it. Asahifuji wants to drive from the right, but his right foot is in the bucket, too far back . . .

You can't beat Chiyonofuji with only your shoulders, dipshit! Where are your legs?!

Instinct saves Chiyonofuji. He feels Asahifuji's mistake. He darts to the left, his feet now on the tawara . . .

Chase him, Asahifuji!

Asahifuji is still finding his feet. Chiyonofuji attacks, tries uwatenage again—the same leaning, twisting, crushing left arm. It doesn't work, but Asahifuji's grip relents. His right hand slips again, off Chiyo's belt. Asahifuji is one-handed again, at least momentarily . . .

The chase continues with Chiyo sliding left, Asahifuji hanging on, each of them one-handed. For a second, Asahifuji is vulnerable, his feet under his chin. But Chiyo doesn't feel it, doesn't drive. The instant passes . . .

A moment at stalemate, then Asahifuji mounts his second offensive. He gets his right hand grip back inside Chiyo's left arm. He braces. Lifts. Turns. Pushes! . . .

No good. Chiyonofuji is too solid. He balances, straightens, saps Asahifuji's power. But as he does, Asahifuji is ready. He was waiting for Chiyo's strength, so he could redirect it. Asahifuji shifts again . . .

Suddenly, he takes his left hand away from the belt, and plunges it inside Chiyonofuji's right arm. Chiyo, recovering his balance, can't counterpunch. He can't stop it . . .

Asahifuji is there. Two hands inside . . .

Morozashi! The death grip.

Asahifuji wanted to end it right then. "I had morozashi," said Asahifuji later. "I remember thinking, 'Now all I have to do is push.'"

He squeezes Chiyonofuji's belt. Push! Chiyonofuji is struggling. His arms are outside and high, holding onto Asahifuji's slippery mawashi like a first-time lover trying to pull his girlfriend's brassiere off over her head . . .

His feet touch the ridge again. Asahifuji is pushing, shifting his hands behind Chiyo's back, his feet clawing at the sand, groping for a position one millimeter higher, just high enough to topple Chiyo backwards . . .

Come on!

Chiyo bends against Asahifuji's body, like a bamboo rod, forestalling what seems inevitable. He can't get out . . .

Jesus Christ, he's out! Look at that!

Leaning only on one shoulder and his right leg, Chiyo simply bulldozes Asahifuji back while gliding to his right. One step. Two steps. Chiyo's off the ridge. Suddenly, Asahifuji's death grip turns out to be just another hug . . .

The crisis past, they trade arm throws, and fail. Asahifuji fights back to morozashi. Chiyonofuji has overpowered Asahifuji with his shoulders repeatedly, but through it all, Asahifuji has never released the deep hold he got at tachiai. He hangs on. He must. He doesn't want to face Chiyonofuji, emptyhanded, on an open dohyo. Not again. Not this time. Not with so much on the line . . .

The match has passed 20 seconds. The crowd is

alternately hushed and shrieking. On one side of the dohyo, Hokutoumi—just beaten by Konishiki—watches Chiyo and gnaws his lip . . .

Feeling Asahifuji tighten morozashi again, Chiyonofuji moves faster. He turns hard, leaning on his left arm, straining to snap Asahifuji's hold. He's on one leg again . . .

Asahifuji feels weakness. He attacks, drives Chiyo to the tawara. The bamboo rod again, bending. Chiyo is cornered, but again, it's too fast. Asahifuji's right hand is loose for, how long?—half a second . . .

It's enough!

Chiyo escapes again. A burst of movement to his left, those shoulders and arms forcing Asahifuji unwillingly back, two effortless strides and they are in the middle of the dohyo, head to head . . .

Goddamn!

Start all over again.

Shonosuke Kimura, the distinguished ref, hovers near, his mouth gaping stupidly . . .

Asahifuji tries pushing again, but fails. He gets beside Chiyo, but Chiyo twists him back to stalemate. Then, lightning. Chiyonofuji commits . . .

This is it.

He yanks Asahifuji to his left side, he plants his left leg between Asahifuji's legs . . .

Chiyonofuji starts to pull . . .

Asahifuji is above him, his morozashi still tight, wrapped around Chiyonofuji's waist with all his might. They crouch, glued together, heaving with fatigue . . .

Chiyonofuji's chin is probably 18 scant inches from the sand. Asahifuji's head, beside his, is almost as close . . .

Chiyo's plan is obvious. He's stronger. This is his best move. Uwatenage. Left hand on top, with a stranglehold on the other guy's mawashi. His feet are wide; he is lower and his balance, if this move works, will survive any pressure Asahifuji can apply from above . . .

If it works . . .

No, he can do it!

Chiyonofuji has been on the defensive for 27 seconds, but now he's home. He's got his hold. He can beat this son of a bitch! . . .

Wait. The other son of a bitch can do it, too! Forget the fact that Chiyo has his beloved uwatenage. He still has to break Asahifuji's morozashi before he can move Asahifuji an inch. Nobody gets morozashi this deep on Chiyo. All Asahifuji has to do is keep leaning on him. Continue to press him down. Crush him to the sand! . . .

When I first watched it, this moment seemed to last for minutes. The two rikishi frozen together, bent over each other, their heads invisible, every sinew in their backs and arms stretched and naked. Only once in a thousand matches does so much desperation radiate so equally from two rikishi as gifted as these. Hold it there! Stay there for an hour! This is too good to end.

There was only one difference. Chiyonofuji, who was underneath except for that one dominant hand, had no options. Asahufuji, somehow, realized he had one.

He let go.

He gave up morozashi, pulled his left hand out from the knot of flesh and slapped it onto the back of Chiyonofuji's neck.

And then Asahifuji committed. He leaned on Chiyo's neck as hard as his left arm could lean, and he threw the rest of himself at Chiyonofuji. If Chiyo could hold his feet, and twist Asahifuji quickly enough, he could throw Asahifuji beneath his body, and land on top.

They begin to fall, together. Toward Chiyo's right. Chiyo pulls, twists at Asahifuji's back. Asahifuji leans . . .

They fall . . .

"I thought I'd lost," said Asahifuji. "I thought my knee touched the dohyo first."

It wasn't that close. Asahifuji's last desperate push closed Chiyonofuji's stance like an accordion. Asahifuji's knees were still spread above the sand, stiff and unsoiled as the Wolf lay curled on the tawara.

No one could challenge the result. Chiyo was down. Sand on his back. Beaten. Asahifuji stood, looking first to Chiyonofuji, seeming to search for an answer in his eyes. Was he offering to help him up? Was he trying to show the respect due a worthy opponent?

He probably was, but such gestures are disdained among the Spartans of sumo. Your only comrades are in your own stable. So Chiyonofuji rose alone, stalked back to his corner and made a sullen exit.

Asahifuji, bewildered ("Didn't my knee touch first?"), crouched for the blessing from Shonosuke Kimura, and received his victory—like a schoolboy shocked by praise from the principal.

"I couldn't think of anything," he said. "I was empty, drained."

Two powerful sumo officials, Futagoyama and

Kokonoe, couldn't think of much either. Asked about the match, and Asahifuji's now unavoidable promotion, they dodged the issue with faint praise.

"It was a great sumo match." said Futagoyama, President of the Sumo Association.

"Good sumo," said Kokonoe.

The mayor of Kizukuri, at least, knew a historic moment when he saw one. "The kid's in the Hall of Fame," he said. "Definitely!"

Chiyonofuji had somehow lost his grace for a moment. He slumped in the passage, on the way to the locker room. "I'm so tired. To get so close, and then to lose . . ."

They asked him about Asahifuji's impending tsunatori. Chiyonofuji said he didn't care what happened to Asahifuji, one way or the other.

"That's somebody else's affair. It has nothing to do with me."

Of course, it had everything to do with him—and this was both his greatness and his burden. He had become an immortal in the midst of his own trials. As long as he wrestled, Chiyonofuji was—for every other rikishi—the ultimate gut check, the final exam. The rite of passage.

Three days later, Asahifuji was promoted.

AFTERWARD

"Keep Up Appearances Whatever You Do"

Fat invites ridicule.

Consider, merely, the expletives we apply to fat people.

Fatso. Slobbo. Glutton. Greedyguts. Pigface. Porky. Wide Load. Whale. Lumpy. Lardass. Baconbutt . . .

No physical anomaly wallows so deep in the mire of our antipathy. "The glutton," said Saadia Gaon in the tenth century, "is like a dog who is never satiated, he becomes disgusting to everyone and, being subject to diarrhea, his body becomes like a sieve . . . "

Gross, huh?

"Obesity," said Joseph O. Kern II in the twentieth century, "is really widespread."

At the disabled, we recoil or we extend pity. Only if provoked by an obstreperous cripple will we search our minds for the appropriate insult. Usually, it's lame.

Tall people we call Stretch, or Slim, or Stringbean—more a matter of acknowledgment than disparagement. Thin people we envy.

And short people? Well, we're not easy on them, but we give 'em a break because they're cute. We might call a short person Shorty, or Squirt, Shrimp, Midge, Halfpint, PeeWee, even Dink. But not "pig," or "tub of shit." We seem to store up our vulgarity for the obese.

Sumo, alone among all the sports in the world, cultivates fat. The fatter in sumo, it seems, the better. Hippos, enormous and crowd-pleasing, advance swiftly up the ranks. But this is a delicate precept, because it so flagrantly flouts the twin virtues of slimness and beauty that represent the modern ideal. Even in Japan, memories of postwar privation are finally fading; healthy fat is losing its cachet. The sunken-cheeked ideal, in the past decade or so, has established itself as aggressively in Tokyo as in New York, Paris, or Venice Beach. Pitted thus against such formidable social mores, sumo teeters perpetually on the brink of burlesque, a wobbling parody of itself. Every rikishi, potentially, is a baggy-pants minstrel without his baggy pants.

With ridicule inherent in the very shape and nature of its athletes, the Sumo Association guards very jealously the dignity of its sport. It's not an easy job.

At the end of every match, there occurs a crisis in dignity, when Blubberbutt triumphs over Moonface, and both of them—usually—end up wallowing in the sand, struggling like tipped-over turtles to right themselves and find their feet. This could turn ludicrous, especially if one of them decides to act up. A triumphant shimmy here, a petulant jiggle there, and suddenly the two noble athletes look like Fatty Arbuckle and Oliver Hardy fighting over a cookie in a Turkish bath.

The Sumo Association's solution is to return to, and enforce, the Code of the Manly Pose. In the aftermath of the match, rikishi follow ritual. They depict the ideal, and they do it in sedate slow motion. They are watched carefully for deviance. Forbidden above all is emotion, because emotion spawns movement—and movement, among fat men, is amusing.

Whether victorious or defeated, the rikishi is stoic and virile. Occasionally, a guy like Trashcan—who tends to lose his momentum and suffer sudden, ridiculous reversals—will vent his frustration by tossing a handful of sand at the dohyo. This is OK, because it is outwardly sincere, self-directed and— best of all—brief. If Trashcan made this a habit, however, he would have to visit the principal's office.

Winners, on the other hand, receive no indulgence. If Asahifuji, for example, had raised a fist and roared with joy after beating Chiyonofuji in Nagoya, he would have instantly placed himself on the verge of expulsion—rather than promotion. Emotionally, sumo is a police state.

"After beating a yokozuna," said Shinko, " you want to jump up and shout. But you have to hold in all that feeling. You're not allowed to show anything."

The Membrane of Sportsmanship

On the other hand—and this is why I admire this mandatory stoicism—sumo is uncluttered by the amateur theatrics that have begun to accompany even the smallest milestones in every meaningless contest in other sports, and which degenerate almost instantly into unintentional self-mockery.

I refer to sack dances, touchdown boogies, finger-pointing, flag-draping, backboard-climbing, pigpiles, high-fives, low-fives, split-level fives, slam dunks over the crossbar, fist-shaking and hugging everybody in sight after another lousy hockey goal, another crummy home run, another measly run-of-the-mill last-second free throw.

I refer to Darryl Strawberry hotdogging around the bases in Game 7 after his only home run in an otherwise putrid World Series performance in 1986. Instead of ashamed, he was obnoxious—and, to their infinite credit, most of America was disgusted.

I refer to the Boston Celtics (and all their subsequent imitators) who besmirched an otherwise heartwarming World Championship in 1984 by waving towels throughout the last quarter, taunting the Lakers and goading to frenzy a crowd that needed no goading.

I exclude those gestures of brotherly communication between teammates that signal approval or thanks—a touch, a pat, a pointed finger, a smiled or a clenched hand, or just a knowing glance. There's a difference between a taunt and a tribute, between showing off and giving notice.

If you're a fan, you know what I mean. And if you're a fan, you share my ambivalence about the showoffs and ham actors who've come to populate professional sports, who feel compelled to amend every simple act of athletic grace with a commercial message about Me. When my own team has the upper hand, I secretly relish the jeer, the sneer, the swagger, the finger that humiliates a beaten foe. But when my side is trailing, or when I have no stake either way, I'm embarrassed by the wretched excess of these juvenile theatrics. And I'm haunted by an old moral dictum about not kicking a man while he's down. I remember the simplicity of a Jim Brown touchdown, a Henry Aaron home run, a slicing Bob Cousy drive to the hoop. No mustard, no fluff, no grandstanding—just execution.

I think most of us—veteran fans—prefer the understated in our athletic heroes, probably because we know that beyond what they do on the field, they don't have much to say. They don't live our lives; they don't know our problems. They are a fortunate, pampered, childlike elite, and so we admire them most when they are strong and silent. John Wayne, not Jerry Lewis. Lou Gehrig, not Billy Martin. And consider how much better we liked Muhammad Ali after he developed a speech impediment!

I wish often we could do something to restore that simplicity and grace, that appreciation for the thing itself without caps and italics. I wish this primarily because sack dances and chocolate thunder are dangerous to the civility of sport. They stretch the thin membrane of sportsmanship, and bring athletes a little closer to the savage that throbs beneath the skin.

The Sumo Association, I think, is keenly sensitive to the fact that the first sumo wrestling was no competition at all—merely a form of human bear-baiting. They wonder how easily it could return to that pass if their jocks began to jiggle and jeer.

It has struck me often that the recent vogue for flouting the fallen foe subjects sports, unwisely, to the vicissitudes of fashion. It isn't tough enough for a strong-armed hillbilly from Dogpatch to pass basketweaving and nostril hygiene 101 at Panhandle Tech, plus learn an entire 200-page playbook and remember the color of his team's jerseys. Nowadays, he has to remember this year's handshake, and whether the trendy touchdown dance this season is closer to a funky chicken or a foxtrot. How can you respect your quarterback if he's still doing last year's finger-flick?

What I've always noted, in the midst of the touchdown boogie, is the aloneness of the performer. For that moment, he divorces himself from the team, from all the athletes on the field, and he celebrates himself. "Hey, look at me! Looka what I did! . . . Look on my six points, ye mighty, and despair!"

In celebrating himself, he reveals too much of himself. He stands a little too naked. His display depicts not strength but weakness, his dependence on a team that worked together to fashion this small private triumph, his fear of letting the act speak for itself, his fear of letting this shining achievement pass too quickly perhaps never to occur again. He intimates his mortality; he reveals the wailing child within the man's body.

"We work," said sportswriter Jimmy Cannon, "in the toy department."

We have seen so many of these prancing displays, these chest-thumping solos, that we no longer trust them. The showoff turns our empathy to contempt.

Maradona, for instance, in the 1990 World Cup Final, joined in his team's effort to stall the game into a 120-minute scoreless tie, in hopes of winning a penalty shootout. It was a travesty that failed. But the crowning shame on this abortion was Maradona, wailing at referees, lamenting his team's well-deserved defeat, and gushing with his crocodile tears.

Tears for a country where he never played soccer—because they couldn't pay him enough.

Nobody likes a showoff, and almost everyone—in his heart—wants to see the son of a bitch get beat.

I've noticed that, even while the modern athlete appears not to understand this truth, our popular art reinforces it. In *The Karate Kid,* director John Avildsen created instant antipathy for hero Daniel's enemies, the Cobra Kai karate jocks, by depicting them as swaggering bullies. And we knew they were bullies, because they swaggered! In the climactic karate tournament, the contrast is nearly overdone. The Cobra Kai dance and strut on the mat, bob and weave, threaten their opponents and, even after they've won, pounce on their opponents, and rain them with insults. Daniel, on the other hand, fights with cool, cautious concentration, from a still and balanced defensive position, repeatedly scoring points on Cobra Kai villains while they shuck and jive.

And the moment after Daniel wins his unlikely victory, Avildsen applied an almost unnoticed but thoughtful directorial touch. While the crowd goes wild and Daniel's supporters rush to the mat to celebrate and hug—and jeer the evil Cobra Kai, Daniel, his concentration unbroken, returns to his

defensive position, holds his balance. Even in certain victory, he is disciplined, silent, humble.

Then, to emphasize the stoic, the quiet, the simple beauty of a man's victory on the playing field, Avildsen cut away from the mob scene, to Mr. Miyagi, the old *sensei.* Miyagi stands apart from the madness, and he nods. His only emotion is the glint of a tear.

Perfect.

The Rite of Withdrawal

Somehow, sometime, sumo's elders accepted this verity, and figured out that it goes double for fat guys. Fat guys, stripped down to g-strings and doing touchdown boogies over other fat guys is not just treacherous—because it could turn the whole sport into a fabric of vendettas and intentional injuries. The bigger problem is that it looks silly.

Mitoizumi (the Asshole), for example, is an immense infant, emotional, demonstrative, unpredictable. He wins ugly—usually by falling awkwardly on top of his opponent—but often. When the match is over, win or lose, Mitoizumi must follow rigid guidelines for his exit from the dohyo. If he loses, he gets to his feet as humbly and quickly as possible, and moves to his side of the dohyo. He waits for the winner to face him. Then, a short bow. Then, Mitoizumi steps off the dohyo, he takes several steps down the aisle, turns, and bows again to everybody in general.

Decorum then requires that he turn on his heel and march impassively down the aisle and into the runway that leads to the locker room. Only when he passes that barrier is any emotion permitted. Then, he can shake his head in disappointment, curse at one of the elves from his sumobeya, toss his fringe in disgust, or kick a water cooler.

If the Asshole wins, he must proceed, with all due gravity, to his side of the dohyo and match the loser's bow. Then, his feelings swelling deliciously beneath his cool exterior, he crouches. The ref (who has just finished another round of screaming) crouches to face Mitoizumi, to whom he offers an envelope that contains his "reward" for victory. Each match has a number of sponsors (like Tokyo Disneyland, Kenji's Bar & Grill) who contribute cash to a winner-take-all pot. The money goes into envelopes and one of the fat elves holds these until the match is over. Then the elf passes the loot to the ref and the ref pays the winner. Tacky, you say? Tackier than Ricky Henderson whining for a contract extension? Come on. Besides, this is a religious thing—Shinto, remember?

Anyway, Mitoizumi has to patiently complete the charade before he gets paid. He's expected to make three distinct chopping movements with his hand— it has some sort of ritual significance—before grabbing the dough. The three chops are usually done with a kind of macho carelessness—as though the victory, and the prize, mean nothing.

"All in a day's work, ref. I'm outa here."

Well, not quite. Next, the Asshole, still maintaining that stony, Spartan gaze (although sucking wind and sweating like a pig), stops at the corner of the dohyo, behind the salt box and the water bucket.

Now, perhaps, he feels the temptation to rub a bruised elbow, straighten his mussed hair, or brush sand from his bod. But he stifles the urge.

Real men don't freshen up.

If, however, his mawashi has been yanked up to his nipples, he has permission to tuck it back under his bellybutton. The Sumo Association approves this much public grooming because the specter of laughter lurks in the disheveled Day-Glo mawashi. It looks silly.

While the fat kid in the corner folds Mitoizumi's fringe and his prize money into a neat package, Mitoizumi takes a drink. He spits it out. He fills the water scoop again. The second scoop is for the next wrestler. After the obligatory stomping and clapping, the next wrestler comes over. Mitoizumi gives him the scoop and bows. The other guy drinks and spits. The fat kid gives Mitoizumi a tiny napkin, which he promptly hands to the other guy, who dabs his mouth.

Mitoizumi is done for the day. He moves up the aisle a step or two, turns, bows, and strides manfully toward the locker room. As he proceeds up the aisle, little ladies and old men scurry to intercept him, patting him giddily on the shoulders as he passes. True to the code, Mitoizumi accepts these caresses without joy or discomfort. Water off a duck's back.

"A man's gotta do what a man's gotta do . . . "

Finally, the runway. Elves surround Mitoizumi. The Asshole can finally be Himself. He grins merrily, slaps hands with one, two, three elves. What, is that a giggle? Is he actually skipping?

It doesn't matter. Nobody can see him now. The rules have protected him from his own exuberance. Forced to march in a narrow groove—even in defiance of his nature—Mitoizumi preserves the dignity of sumo and all his fellow fatsos. By following the rules, Mitoizumi partakes (although imperfectly) of that ironic, endearing grace that fat men exude when they conquer the absurdity of their shape. As often as we laugh cruelly at Tweedledum and Tweedledee and all their roly-roly peers, we respond with incongruous esteem to those fat men whose suavity transcends their obesity.

In the presence (or memory) of certain swollen eminences, we simply do not laugh. Sidney Greenstreet, Orson Welles, Charles Laughton. Babe Ruth! John Madden, Louis VI, Khrushchev. Kate Smith, Pavarotti, Mahalia Jackson, Mickey Lolich. The piano Fatses: Waller & Domino. Colonel Sanders. Chesterton and Hitchcock.

Konishiki!

The ultimate portrait of the impeccable, intimidating fat man was Jackie Gleason, portraying Minnesota Fats in *The Hustler*. When Fast Eddy called him "fat man" with a voice of contempt, it came to the ear with the resonance of awe. This is the respect the Sumo Association imposes on an unwilling public. It shrouds its giants in exceeding gravity, dresses them in the classic simplicity of a bygone, romantic time: *yukata*, the simple robe; *obi*, the plain belt; *geta*, the wooden shoes of the rice farmer. When they wrestle (barefoot), the only garment, the mawashi, is a *fundoshi*—antediluvian underwear.

And it all works.

The aftermath, the ritual of withdrawal, in sumo, is timeless and funereal. We see rikishi not as individual combatants, with style and personality, calm or excitable, loud or reticent. They are, in the Sumo Association's prescription, elements in a procession, concealing themselves behind a mask of deportment.

"Keep up appearances," said Pecksniff, "whatever you do."

If you let them act according to their own devices, they would, alas, act like children. Silly children. Fat children. Embarrassing children.

Of course, there are breaks in this solid front. According to the rules, for instance, it is bad form to offer one's hand to a beaten opponent. As a Real Man, one must disdain the fallen warrior and leave him to lift himself by his own bootstraps like another Real Man (even though he doesn't have any boots and he's rolling on the ground like a beached porpoise). Now and then, however, an impulse of unbridled compassion seizes a rikishi. He reaches out to help the loser. And once in a blue moon, without considering his dignity, his machismo or the good of the Association, the loser accepts that kindness and they pass that most forbidden of sentiments in sumo—fellowship toward athletes from another club.

Even more often, there are acts of sportsmanship—both good and bad—that are a little more subtle. After a rikishi has been driven across the ridge in defeat, his back to the audience, and his momentum uncontrollable, he is obviously vulnerable. The winner can choose to send him flying—perhaps to injury—with an extra nudge. Or he can save him by simply planting his feet and holding on. Takatoriki (Dangerous Dan), who matches Mitoizumi in immaturity and entertainment value, usually chooses the former—heaving his opponent into the audience and then glowering at the tangle of bodies he has created. Slightly more often, however, a rikishi will relent and hold on, saving a beaten foe from the fall. The Sumo Association overlooks both gestures.

The Interview

The place where post-match etiquette faces its most serious challenge, and—ironically—enjoys its brightest spotlight, is in the inimitable NHK sumo interview. These occur only after the mighty have fallen, when a lesser wrestler defeats a giant. Everyone who beats a yokozuna (except another yokozuna) gets interviewed, and almost everyone who beats Konishiki gets interviewed. These interviews, if they were entirely free-wheeling and candid, would certainly provide the Sumo Association with ample opportunity for embarrassment. However, they are conducted by NHK "sportscasters," who have two overwhelming priorities. The first is to advance and glorify the Sumo Association. The second is to ingratiate themselves with the rikishi. Both purposes are served by asking questions that would not confuse an orangutan.

In fact, the ideal sumo interview reminds the viewer of an interview with a lesser primate. In recent times, the ideal interview subject is Akinoshima—who is, thank goodness, not nearly as tragically stupid as he seems when interviewed after wrestling. If he actually were that dim, he would be in an institution somewhere, wearing a bib at every meal and playing with his toes.

But we'll get to Akinoshima momentarily. First, one must understand that to "interview" a sumo wrestler is essentially a contradiction in principles—because this guy, by administrative fiat, is supposed to be the strong silent (verging on catatonic) type.

However, since an outright gag rule would peg the Sumo Association as obstructionist, most rikishi have learned an interview style that gives the average listener a renewed appreciation for silence. The end of a sumo interview is always a relief.

The characteristics of a truly accomplished sumo interviewee include the following techniques:

• A deep, rasping, breathy voice. Picture a throat cancer victim attempting to place an obscene phone call.

• Breathing into the mike, deafeningly. Even when a rikishi has mastered the Voice of the Cancer Victim, some of what he says might still be intelligible if one listens carefully. Apparently to prevent this possibility, NHK never puts one of those sponge-rubber baffles onto its microphones, thus allowing interviewees to smother, with an ear-rending gasp, every monosyllable they utter. The world's record for gasping thunderously into a mike during a sumo interview belongs to the unchallenged master, Kotogaume, who did it 33 times in one 60-second interview. Not a word he said could be understood.

• Face-wiping. Even after a one-second "matador," your typical rikishi interviewee will arrive at an NHK interview gushing with sweat, hoarse with exhaustion and sucking wind like a chain smoker in the Boston Marathon. So he brings his towel along. This allows him to cover his face fifteen or twenty times in the course of the interview, placing the towel over his mouth with every answer—usually just after whoofing into the microphone.

• Stupid questions, stupid answers. Roughly 90 percent of all questions asked to athletes by TV interviewers in Japan begin with the phrase, "How did you feel? . . ." This is an approach much approved by virtually everyone in the sports world, from commissioners to athletes to the waterboy, because it's always something an orangutan could handle, with a one-word response.

• No vowels. One sign of true manliness in Japan, besides speaking in a guttural rumble that makes Don Corleone, by comparison, sound like Minnie Mouse, is to eschew vowels. Japan's foremost vowel droppers are sumo wrestlers. And since vowel sounds do exist in Japanese, the virtually unintelligible responses gurgled forth in a sumo interview become a linguistic conundrum more appropriate to anthropologists than sports fans. Let's drop in, for instance, on Akinoshima, as he's interviewed after yet another stirring defeat of Konishiki. His eyes are glassy, his body drenched with sweat, his mouth slack. One wonders if he's alive, until the microphone inches closer to his face and picks up the telltale roar of his breath.

Akinoshima wipes his face, apparently to no effect. Rivulets spurt from every pore.

The interviewer cringes to Akinoshima's right, barely visible on the edge of the TV screen. There is something in the constriction of his voice that tells us he's smiling as he tries to talk. A Japanese sportscaster who can't grin and talk simultaneously never makes it to the bigtime. He begins:

NHK: "Akinoshima, that was a wonderful match. One of the great moments in sumo history. I was personally moved and overwhelmed by the drama of such great sumo. Congratulations. What can I say? You were wonderful! What a future you have! I hope I have children who grow up to be just like you and that they have identical children and that their children are also just like you. Now, excuse me, big guy, but I must ask you something, please, and I hope I'm not prying, because if I am, I'm terribly sorry. I'll ask a different question. Or I'll just go away. What I want to know, please, if you don't mind, is: How did you feel before the match?"

AKINOSHIMA: (Gasping into the mike as he wipes his face.) "Rr."

[Translation: "Rr."]

NHK: "Oh, I forgot to say—how could it have slipped my mind? What a blunder. I'm really sorry, I hope you'll forgive me—I forgot to congratulate not only you, but your brilliant oyakata, Fujishima, who prepared you so flawlessly for this wonderful effort. Listen, can you tell me what Fujishima told you before today's match?"

AKINOSHIMA: *(Wipe. Gasp. Roar. A long, thoughtful pause. Several whoofs.)* "Wsrmsht'."

["I can't remember."]

NHK: "Really? Well, how did you feel as he was passing these instructions along?"

AKINOSHIMA: *(Gasp. Roar. Wipe.)* "Wsrmsht'."

["I don't remember that, either."]

NHK: "Fascinating! Great! Well, then, how did you feel at the moment that Konishiki got migi-yotsu and started driving you off the dohyo. That was a pretty scary moment, wasn't it?"

AKINOSHIMA: *(Wipe. Gasp.)* "S' ds' ne."

["Yup."]

NHK: "And then, you must have felt better when he tripped on his own feet and started to fall, huh?"

AKINOSHIMA: *(Silence, save for the rhythmic roaring of the mike, the sound of sweat trickling gently 'twixt valleys of flab.)*

NHK: "Well, of course. Then, when he actually fell, aided by that brilliant move you made, by getting out of his way, then, tell me, what were your feelings at that triumphant moment? Were you glad? Did you think it was over?"

AKINOSHIMA: "Rr."

NHK: "Well, Akinoshima, as usual, we are amazed not only by your sumo, but by your eloquence off the dohyo. Before you leave, if I may indulge you with one more probing question, please, excuse my intrusion, but I'm sure your fans want to know— now think about this one—How do you feel about tomorrow's match?"

AKINOSHIMA: *(Gasp. Roar. Trickle. Wipe.)* "Gmbrms."
["Gonna try hard."]

NHK: "What a trouper. Well, we wish you the very best of the very best luck and we hope you do your best. And congratulations again, and we will all be grateful, for a long time, that you troubled to come back here and grace us with this unforgettable interview. Thank you, big guy, thank you. Sorry to have bothered you. Thanks for coming. Sorry. Thanks. Sorry. Thanks again. Sorry."

AKINOSHIMA: *(Wipe. Gasp. Roar. A desultory bow. Gasp. Whoof.)* "Rgto gzms."
["Thanks."]

As wretched as most sumo interviews are, there are notable exceptions, especially when the rikishi involved is too happy to follow the rules. During the best basho of his career, for example, Wakasegawa

(Paddington) got his first interview ever, and he was full of engaging, voluble insights on himself and his matches. Many ex-*gakusei-zumo* (former collegiate rikishi) speak thoughtfully and articulately. Chiyonofuji (who might be the smartest man in Japan who never went to high school) is also unconventional. He speaks in a normal, slightly high and boyish, voice, jokes with the interviewer and has a gracious talent for turning the typical stupid questions into revealing answers.

These exceptions prove the wisdom of the rule. The Sumo Association's vow of silence is a stroke of genius, because it fosters sumo's finest virtue—its wordless, instinctual simplicity. Its athletes are drilled to a level of insensibility that makes it difficult for them to say what they did—even in the first moment afterwards—or how they did it.

There is eloquence in allowing the deed to speak for itself. There is wisdom in restraining the doer from embellishing the deed with word or action. There is class in preventing him from gloating, explaining or moralizing in retrospect.

The great rikishi and the great gunfighter are kindred.

You remember what happened after Shane snuffed all the outlaws? No shouting, right? No flourish. No swagger. The deed is done, there is nothing to say. Alan Ladd pauses only a moment to consider Jack Palance's corpse. His face reveals nothing; we might read it as we wish.

The little boy, Joey—who is a dramatic device installed by director George Stevens to elicit Shane's thoughts—does the post-gunfight interview and squeezes out enough moral lessons to pack a small missal: "Thou shalt not kill" . . . "Honor thy father and mother". . . "Do your thing and keep your mouth shut". . . Original sin and predestination ("A man has to be what he is, Joey.") . . . Gun control. . . Social security. All this in 73 words. Shane also manages to articulate the sumo philosophy of injuries: bleed quietly and avoid medical help.

No need to ask any more questions. Shane's silence is his soliloquy. Having gently shed the intrusive Joey, Shane slips away. Like a weary rikishi shlepping toward the locker room, he rides off— morally ambiguous and deaf to the child's adulation— into the hills.

10

THE BASHO BOOGIE

If the individual match, which I've belabored in the previous six chapters, is sumo's microcosm, then the basho is its macrocosm. It is the universe that integrates all the little fights and makes sense of them.

In a basho's schedule lies the flow of sumo—its rhythm, its ordeal. The Sumo Association's finest and subtlest achievement is its refinement of the fifteen-day struggle. The schedule is a work of intellect and balance, a kind of philosophical fabric, that has few parallels in sport. It is, moreover, a kind of monastic trial in which most everything is foreordained, in which even the surprises are preceded by their shadows. Once a fan has sensed the flow of the basho, he can feel the unexpected coming, in the moments before it unfolds.

Although seemingly a crescendo, the basho is more accurately a loose composition, within which improvisation induces infinite variety—a kind of softspoken jazz played by fat men. Within the composition, the schedule dances up and down the scale of rikishi and through a range of outcomes. This is the melody. The bass line, thumping steadily beneath these flowing notes, is the hierarchy, the rankings of rikishi that determine who wrestles whom, and when.

To perceive the sense of the basho's rhythm, you have to understand its strange purpose. The individual rikishi does not necessarily pursue the same goal from match-to-match, and he must be perpetually sensitive to the "higher goals" sought—through him—by his sumobeya and for the sumo world at large.

For a rikishi in a match—most of the time—winning is the objective. Beat the other guy. However, most rikishi learn that the institution of sumo is not well-served by practitioners who harbor a singleminded and impolite passion for victory after victory. Rikishi learn that, over the course of a basho, winning isn't everything, or the only thing. In many cases, it's not even something. The real objective, for all but an elite handful of rikishi in sumo's top division, is not to win the basho championship—or even contend for it. What most of the guys are shooting for is *kachikoshi.*

Kachikoshi is eight wins and seven losses, one match above .500. In most sports, this—a winning percentage of .533—denotes mediocrity and spurs the earnest jock to work harder and get better. For the overwhelming majority of sumo wrestlers, it is the definition of success. As long as a rikishi makes kachikoshi, he is assured of creeping upward in the ranks.

In all things, moderation.

The opposite of kachikoshi is *makekoshi,* (7–8 or worse)—which isn't good, but, well, it's no catastrophe either. Usually, makekoshi gets a rikishi demoted to a level where his opponents aren't quite so tough, and so his next kachikoshi comes easier. Once he's got Victory No. 8 in a basho, a rikishi can relax, maybe help out a few other guys with their kachikoshi. In sumo, kachikoshi is Miller Time. If winning a few more matches looks a little too strenuous, or the prospect of success seems too scary, nobody faults a guy for slacking off. In sumo, 8–7 is just about the same as 11–4—and much more sociable.

In practical terms, this means that, among the forty rikishi in the first—makuuchi—division in any given basho, there are only three, perhaps four, occasionally five, genuine contenders for the yusho. The other three dozen are all aiming at the same golden mean: kachikoshi.

To dream the possible dream, to avoid the unbeatable foe . . .

Banzuke: Confucian Confusion

Of course, the Sumo Association does not precede each basho by publishing a list of "real contenders" and obligatory also-rans. Their rankings, printed before each basho in a beautiful hand-lettered poster called the *banzuke,* follow a formula that dates at least to the seventeenth century. Below the top two ranks of yokozuna and ozeki, a rikishi's status can really fluctuate according to his previous basho record.

After kachikoshi, he goes up; makekoshi, he goes down.

Yokozuna can never be demoted (although if they stink up the joint repeatedly, they have to retire). Ozeki can only be demoted after two straight makekoshi.

Remember the ranks for rikishi in makuuchi? From top to bottom, they are yokozuna (the pinnacle), ozeki, sekiwake, komusubi and maegashira.

It's customary to refer to this hierarchy of ranks in sumo as "Confucian," because it was Confucius' idea that civilization properly forms itself into an interlocking hierarchy of social stations, with people at each level owing obligations to, and receiving indulgence from, those above and those below, a construct often described as "filial piety." "Confucian" is one of the standard buzzwords Westerners use to explain almost everything that happens in Japan. This especially applies to lists. The banzuke is a list; ergo, it must be Confucian.

For instance, in my Tokyo apartment building, the lobby is located on the fourth floor, a fact that never fails to confuse visitors. They ask why this is so.

"Well," I explain, "this is common in Japan, because of the influence of hierarchical Confucian thinking, and the significance of the concept of the 'Fourth Level,' or 'yonkai.'"

Usually, this satisfies them. The real reason is that my building is on the side of a hill, which requires that there are more floors on the downslope than on the upslope. But this would take a great deal of explaining, probably with a lot of math and physics—and questions I couldn't answer. Confucius saves me the aggravation.

Actually, the sumo ranks aren't Confucian. They're Darwinist. This is because, in day-to-day life, rikishi don't put much stock in filial piety. It's a one-way street. The kids in the lower ranks kiss ass, and the guys up above kick it. The mechanism that determines this pecking order is performance—how well you did in the last basho and how far you got promoted. Occasionally, a really virtuoso bootlicker can cling to his bed and board in the sumobeya despite a lousy record as a wrestler. But sooner or later, he has to make kachikoshi, or look for another line of work.

If you look at your average banzuke, even if you can't read the Japanese, it isn't hard to figure out that the upper-ranked wrestlers' names are written real big, and the names shrink as you go down the list. Generally, it's correct to assume that rikishi tend to be scheduled against guys whose names are the same size. But you can't count on this. Sumo Association schedulers have both a system and a playful curiosity ("Don't you wonder what would happen if this guy fought that guy?"). Basho are full of crossovers, from level to level—which make it possible for lesser wrestlers to test themselves against the studs, and maybe move up.

To make this happen, the Sumo Association applies an unwritten code of "practical rankings." For instance, because there are only 10 to 12 rikishi in the upper four ranks of sumo, a rikishi at this level has to wrestle down, among the maegashira, in as many as six matches per basho. Which six guys does he fight? Do those six guys have to take on all the rikishi on the top?

The answer lies, usually, in where each rikishi lands on the banzuke. Before a rikishi sets eyes on the schedule (which, as you recall, is fixed only two days in advance of each day's wrestling), the banzuke gives him a broad notion of how tough his opponents will be in the coming two weeks, and what his expectations ought to be.

One thing he barely thinks about is which "team" he's on. Sometime back in sumo's dim middle ages, the elders divided rikishi into "East" and "West" teams—based on where they came from. It's doubtful—in this essentially man-to-man sport—whether anybody ever really had much team spirit for the East Side or the West Side. But by the 1950s, there wasn't even a remnant of team play. Nowadays, the East/West split is an empty form. However, it is good to know that, for rikishi of equal rank on the traditional scale—for instance, maegashira No. 7—the East guy is considered slightly superior to the West guy.

With one exception noted below, you may disregard this East/West business entirely.

The Real Ranks: Upper Echelon

The banzuke divides the upper ranks into two groups. At the top are yokozuna, and below are the three *sanyaku* ranks: ozeki, sekiwake, and komusubi. They all wrestle each other, but don't be fooled by mere status. Even in these lofty climes, the objectives of individual rikishi vary. Remember, winning isn't everything!

First of all, in terms of sheer quality, the only

difference between a yokozuna and an ozeki is time and politics. Politics kept Asahifuji out of yokozuna for years, but in time, they let him join because he kept embarrassing yokozuna. Onokuni, although entrenched at yokozuna for years, was a panda of a different color. Except for an occasional spasm of good health and enthusiasm, his record was worse than most ozeki, and he hardly ever challenged for a yusho.

THE ELITE. In essence, then, yokozuna and ozeki comprise a single class best referred to simply as the Elite. The Elite breaks down, in a practical sense, into two classes, which can be measured, essentially, according to desire. These are:

• THE PENNANT RACE, which comprises only those wrestlers who are seriously competing for the tournament title and are athletically capable of winning it; and

• THE GRAVY TRAIN, which includes those members of the Elite who just don't have what it takes to win the championship—victims of the Peter Principle who have reached their level of incompetence and settled in with no higher aspirations.

In the 1990 Nagoya Basho, for example, the Elite broke down into five rikishi in the Pennant Race—Chiyonofuji, Hokutoumi, Asahifuji, Konishiki, and Kirishima, and two rikishi on the Gravy Train—Onokuni and Hokutenyu. There was a good possibility that as many as three of the Pennant Racers, Chiyo, Hokutoumi, and especially Konishiki, might switch over to the Gravy Train within a year. Konishiki had been on it before.

Below the Elite, two sanyaku ranks, sekiwake and

komusubi, present the most brutal schedules in sumo.

THE TIGHTROPE. A sekiwake is neither here nor there. He's better than almost everybody down below, the maegashira, and he's gotten through komusubi—otherwise known as the Meatgrinder— perhaps several times. His schedule includes every- one in the upper ranks, and he scores the occasional upset among the Elite. But he's a kachikoshi kinda guy, just trying to stay where he is. It's a crowded tightrope; there are guys approaching from both ends, trying to push him off.

Rikishi reach the Tightrope and stay there for a while usually because they have a very effective technique, or some physical feature, that makes them tough to beat. Kotogaume, sumo's most dangerous Butterball, for instance, is built low to the ground and incredibly dense. He lingered at sekiwake for six straight basho in 1989-90. Terao, a fanatic battler who can overwhelm almost anyone for a period of five seconds, established himself in 1990 as a Tightrope level rikishi and spent five basho there. He actually took the place of his brother Sakahoko, a morozashi specialist who clung to the Tightrope for almost two years, 'til an arm injury ruined his form and reversed his fortunes in mid- 1989. None of these three rikishi had much hope of ever moving any further up.

When a sekiwake (like Kotogaume, Terao, Sakahoko) can't expand his repertoire in response to the intense demands of the Tightrope, gravity will get him by and by—with a stop (possibly even a recovery) in the Meatgrinder on the way down. Kirishima was the rare Tightroper who was still learning and growing when he reached sekiwake. For him, the Tightrope was a one-basho pause on his way to the Elite.

But for most, the Tightrope is more likely a place from which to fall. And to fall means into the next lower designation, komusubi—not a pleasant fate. I refer to this detention cell for rising and falling rikishi simply as . . .

THE MEATGRINDER. The Sumo Association uses the Meatgrinder for three distinct and useful purposes:

1) To punish maegashira wrestlers who have succeeded excessively in matches at the lower levels, perhaps by racking up a 10–5 or 11–4 record from some lowly rung like maegashira No. 8. The Meatgrinder is the schedule-master's way of saying, "OK, smartass, you think you're hot shit? We have a few guys we'd like you to meet."

2) As an entrance exam for rising stars, to see if they're ready for prime time. When a promising wrestler has been seasoned in the maegashira ranks for a while, and he has a good previous basho, and there's an opening at komusubi (there's almost always an opening at komusubi), they put him in the Meatgrinder. There isn't much difference, in this respect, between a test and punishment—except in terms of expectations. It's a punishment when the Sumo Association knows a rikishi will get creamed in the Meatgrinder. It's an exam when the rikishi has a chance to survive. Even if he doesn't make kachikoshi, the Meatgrinder is the rising star's chance to upset an ozeki, or even a yokozuna, and

impress some people. If he can do that, he'll be back for a second chance.

For instance, in January, 1989, Kirishima—then 29 years old and essentially aimless in his sumo career, despite a lot of talent—made the Meatgrinder. In succession, on the first five days, he wrestled Onokuni (yokozuna), Hokutenyu (ozeki), Konishiki (ozeki), Chiyonofuji (yokozuna) and Hokutoumi (yokozuna). He lost every match and fell apart at the seams, putting on sumo's sorriest performance of the year. His 1–14 record wasn't as good as it looks on paper. This was the sort of experience that makes a guy look back on his life and ask some serious questions.

Kirishima, however, found answers. From that nadir, he somehow turned his career around. It took him only 'til July '89 to get back to the Meatgrinder, this time going 7–8. That makekoshi included a three-day spectacular—at the beginning of the basho—when he beat Chiyonofuji, Hokutenyu and Konishiki in succession. By December, Kirishima was back in the Meatgrinder, where he did something few rikishi have ever done. He survived two straight basho in the Meatgrinder, with records of 10–5 and 11–4, and he beat the Elite eight times.

3) The Meatgrinder also serves as a safety net for sekiwake on their way down after makekoshi. The schedule is little different, but after losing at sekiwake, komusubi is the falling rikishi's second chance before he gets kicked down among the maegashira. Of six rikishi who had winning records in the Meatgrinder between January '89 and July '90, four were former sekiwake.

How tough is the Meatgrinder? It means you have

to wrestle every rikishi ranked above you—first—before you get a break with the guys underneath. And your very first matches are the Elite. By the time you get to the lower-ranked wrestlers, your form and self-esteem are so shattered that beating anyone—including your grandmother—is beyond your wildest dreams. The Meatgrinder is as high as most rikishi ever go. In almost every case, it's a ticket down.

Including Kirishima's exceptional two basho in November '89 and January '90, when his Meatgrinder record was 21–9, the total record for Meatgrinder victims, from January '89 through July '90 was 113–178 (.388). Six rikishi went up, 13 went down and one (Kirishima) stood pat.

The Real Ranks: Down Below

Kirishima was Cinderella. Most of sumo consists of ugly stepsisters, otherwise known as maegashira.

In traditional Sumo Association terms, maegashira are ranked in neat, descending order from maegashira No. 1 through maegashira No. 15. In fact, this big category just below komusubi breaks down into three groups that I separate by difficulty of schedule. These classifications are Cannon Fodder, the Fish Tank and the Border Patrol. Here's how they break down.

CANNON FODDER. The big guys up-top (yokozuna through komusubi) all need little guys down below to pick on, especially in the first half of the basho. The Sumo Association picks out seven of them. These guys—cannon fodder—are almost always the top seven rikishi below the Meatgrinder, a platoon composed of East maegashira No. 1–4 and West maegashira No. 1–3.

The West maegashira No. 4 has a much softer schedule than his East Side counterpart—showing that there is, yes, one item of significance in this East/West nonsense. However, West maegashira No. 4 isn't necessarily out of cannon range, because when a rikishi ranked above him—anyone from yokozuna to maegashira No. 3—gets hurt and quits the tourney, he's the guy first in line to fill in the gap upstairs. In some tournaments, with a lot of upper-rank withdrawals, the Grim Reaper of scheduling can reach all the way down to maegashira No. 5.

THE FISH TANK. My old friend Schuster was a high school wrestler, and during the season, he suffered almost fatally from two anxieties: l) keeping his weight at 138 pounds, and 2) his next opponent. Schuster's record hovered eternally around kachikoshi, so he had a philosophical grasp of his own limitations. He knew which opponents he could never beat in a million tries, and the ones against whom he dared to envision victory. In a way, Schuster was a kind of human benchmark for wrestling competence; when he saw a guy whom he knew that even he could whip, Schuster found it difficult to respect him. He applied to such opponents wrestling's most scornful putdown: "fish."

Schuster, if he had gone on to a sumo career, would be Cannon Fodder, and he would beat most of the rikishi below that level. In our house, we've adopted the Schuster designation spontaneously and logically. For instance, Junko would say to me, on Day 4, "So, who's Chiyonofuji got today?"

I look it up in the schedule published every day in the *Japan Times* and see Jingaku pitted against the Wolf.

"A fish."

Rolls right off the tongue.

Hence, a group of about twenty rikishi below Cannon Fodder comprise the Fish Tank. Fish have pretty easy schedules, wrestling among themselves and competing mainly to collect their kachikoshi.

However, despite its lowly place in the makuuchi scheme of things, the Fish Tank is a source of endless fascination for the fan. Here is sumo's melting pot. Here we find old pugs, pushed from the lofty regions of sanyaku and destined never to rise again. But you dare not write them off. These are foxy old bastards; given the soft schedule that is the blessing of the Fish Tank, they can outwit younger wrestlers, take turns picking each other off, and survive.

Here, too, are the youngsters, fresh up from juryo with stars in their eyes, spring in their muscles and a pink flush on their pudgy little cheeks. The Fish Tank is where they get baptized into the brutal tachiai and sneaky tricks of the old reprobates in the bigtime.

Here also are the yo-yo's, both youngsters and veterans, so-called because they bounce up and down the ranks of the Fish Tank. They score kachikoshi in a basho and move up a few notches, maybe even within range of the cannons. Then, makekoshi, once—even twice—until they're down far enough to find fish dumber and weaker than they are are. Then, kachikoshi and back up again.

One of my favorite yo-yo's, who finally yo-yoed down to juryo in 1990, was a feisty little toad named

Koboyama, whose only move was a desperate, bowling-ball lunge at tachiai. In the twilight of his career, Koboyama was *poisson du poissons,* hopelessly overmatched every time he stepped on the dohyo. Most rikishi could beat him in their sleep. And still, Koboyama hung on, getting impossible mileage out of that ridiculous charge. He had a sixth sense for outsmarting greenhorn kids—who would give him one look, smirk, blow their concentration, and lose.

The Fish Tank also provides a resting place for good athletes who fall from grace through injury or inattention. Tochinowaka (Big Al), for instance, is so busy admiring himself that he often leaves his brains in his jockstrap for two or three consecutive basho. When he finds himself treading water in the Fish Tank, he finally wakes up, feasts on shlemiels and starts his way back up toward the Meatgrinder.

Sakahoko, who wrenched his left arm badly in summer 1989 after nine basho on the Tightrope, landed in the Fish Tank and spent most of the next year there, convalescing and slowly regaining his health. He was obviously frustrated with the mediocrity of his opponents and performances after being so long in the upper echelon. But he was also secure; with only sardines on his schedule, he could win at will and play yo-yo while struggling to regain his form.

Almost every basho, one fish gets hot and starts devouring other fish so voraciously that suddenly, in the second week of the basho, he finds himself listed among the tournament leaders—alongside the Wolf, Asahifuji, Konishiki! For instance, in the 1990 Spring (March) Basho, Kushimaumi, a promising Hippo, was rock bottom, maegashira No. 14. He went through his first ten matches at 9–1, at which point the Sumo Association changed his category from fish to cannon fodder, and set him up against Kirishima.

And he won! OK, try again, against Konishiki. This time, Kushimaumi couldn't pull the upset, and then Terao beat him, and then Big Al. He ended up at 10-5, an impressive Fish Tank record, and he got one of the three consolation prizes, the Fighting Spirit Award, that the Sumo Association gives to its upstarts.

THE BORDER PATROL. The one thing that no makuuchi wrestler wants is demotion to juryo. The rikishi who falls back to the second division invariably finds his comeback much harder than his initial ascension to makuuchi. The reasons for this, I think, lie within the Sumo Association and, perhaps more significantly, within the rikishi's mind.

The Sumo Association, like any other showbiz organization, loves new blood. Management wants to feed fresh young faces to the public. So, when all other measures are equal and the Sumo Association has a choice between lifting an old fish or a rookie from juryo to makuuchi, the committee tends to lean toward the kid. In order to get back to makuuchi, after slipping to juryo, an oldtimer must clearly dominate his younger (stronger, prettier, quicker, eagerer) opponents in juryo. He needs knockouts, not split decisions.

The other barrier to comebacks is the mind, a sense of ennui that seems to overwhelm and defeat older rikishi who've dropped a division. I've seen competent rikishi, perhaps hindered by nagging injuries, fall to juryo—where, even hurt, they are superior to most of their opponents. But they don't show it. They crumble in their first juryo tournament and flounder for a year or more in the second division. Some make it back, some just settle in to juryo for the rest of their careers. And some just continue to plummet, down to makushita (the third division), and down and down, until embarrassment hounds them into retirement.

The better alternative, of course, is not to get caught in that dangerous spiral. The makuuchi wrestlers who face that threat are the rikishi at the bottom of the first division—the Border Patrol. Depending on the number of rikishi in the upper ranks, the Border Patrol guys might be numbered anywhere from maegashira No. 12 to maegashira No. 16. When Kushimaumi put on that terrific show in the 1990 March Basho, he did it, actually, from the bottom of the Fish Tank, as a Border Patrolman. Typically, the Border Patrol includes two young guys just pushed up from juryo, and two older rikishi who screwed up in the last basho and stand at the crossroads of their careers.

I usually don't waste much sympathy on the young up-and-comers. Frequently, their promotion to makuuchi is premature. Few people expect them to stick on their first trip to makuuchi, and a lot of us want to see the bloated little snots get their ears boxed before being shipped back down to the minors for a little more seasoning. If they're good, they'll learn from their stint in the Border Patrol and return in a few basho. If they're not good enough, at least they've had a cup of coffee in the Bigs.

The real drama in the Border Patrol is with the old guys—like Koboyama—making, maybe, their last stand against age and flab and " . . . the heartache and the thousand natural shocks/That flesh is heir to . . . "

"Come on, you old tub! Hang in there!"

Occasionally, a different sort of oldtimer is recruited into the Border Patrol. The Sumo Association (because they're old guys, too, and they know how it feels) occasionally spot a juryo journeyman who's been hauling his ass up to the mat every day for twenty years but he's never going to be good enough. A lot of innings, but no zip. So they send him up to the Show, anyway. Even though the Border Patrol is makuuchi's softest schedule, he ends up getting punched out and sent back. But so what? He's been there. When he retires, he will retire at the highest rank of his career—maegashira—and his pension will be a little bigger.

When you're watching a basho, enjoy the Pennant Race. But keep an eye on the Border Patrol, where the rhythm and the drama of sumo throbs just as deep, just as hungrily, and a little more poignantly.

The Weight of Concentration

Regardless of where in the pecking order a rikishi finds himself, he faces a psychological pressure that's unique among all the sports in the world. Remember that, in 15 days of the tournament, a typical rikishi spends only about a minute and a half actually fighting.

Each day, when he steps on the dohyo, he bends under the weight of 24, 48, 72 hours of anticipation. He's been wrestling this match in his head for two days. And he knows that whatever he has imagined will be completely different from what really happens—

and he's going to have maybe a half-second to recognize that and react to it. In 15 days of relentless tension six times a year, the weight of concentration never lightens. And let's try to remember these aren't exactly the world's sharpest intellects. Even among sumo's brightest, a split second break, a blink of inattention, can destroy a match, lose a yusho.

In the 1988 Kyushu (November) Basho, Chiyonofuji entered the final match at 14–0, against Onokuni. Chiyo was on the longest winning streak—53 straight matches—in modern sumo history. He'd already clinched the yusho, so this win was only to extend the streak and to rack up another undefeated basho. Chiyonofuji should have won, but something happened during the Sumotori Rag. For one blink, just before he stepped out for tachiai, Chiyo's eyes darted. It was an odd, noticeable flicker, because Chiyo was consistently trancelike at tachiai. That flicker betrayed a blur in Chiyo's focus. Some distraction—perhaps the winning streak itself—had diverted him from the business at hand, which was to wrestle this one match, right now, this minute, against this opponent.

Onokuni beat Chiyonofuji and ended the streak— thus earning, unwittingly, the undying resentment of the Sumo Association. But Chiyonofuji recognized his error and later admitted that he had, just that once, lost touch with the lesson, the motto, the bass line of sumo: "One day at a time."

Lose the beat, lose the game.

Shinko, when I spoke with him, talked about how hard it is to keep the beat, because there is so little actual wrestling and so much waiting. It begins to weigh on a rikishi as the basho drags on and all that first-day adrenaline disperses. Between Day 6 and Day 10, said Shinko, concentration falters—and this is when Elite rikishi start suffering upsets to lesser wrestlers.

Then, if you've blown several matches and fallen out of the running, recovering the old karma gets even harder. The Meatgrinder, above all, pulverizes concentration. It throws a rikishi against almost impossible odds through the first entire week of the basho, crushes hope, and inevitably breaks his daily discipline. Few rikishi manage to find the beat again. If they do, they usually win a few matches at the end of the basho and come out of the Meatgrinder with at least a few shreds of pride intact.

Good Basho, Bad Basho

One of the issues raised among sumo nerds toward the end of each basho is whether or not this was a "good basho." I thought this a strange question when first I heard it, and I haven't much changed my opinion.

What I didn't see was how all these disparate events, these hundreds of fights among dozens of wrestlers at four or five different levels spread over more than two weeks, could be so blithely categorized. Since then, however, I've derived some sense of what's meant by this "good basho." Sumo nerds (who hie pretty faithfully to the Sumo Association outlook on these subjective points) apparently think a basho is "good" if the climax conforms to the Confucian crescendo envisioned by the boys in charge. Ideally, attention in the last days of the basho centers on the battle for the yusho among the yokozuna—who, by this time, should have disdainfully tossed aside all of their lesser opponents, which hardly ever happens. But never mind reality. A basho, apparently, is diminished if that favorite son of the masses—the underdog—pulls off a surprise and whips the Elite.

The Sumo Association blushes (needlessly) whenever one of its Elite gets ambushed. This is an interesting outlook, which finally gets us down to the Confucian nitty-gritty. Some pigs are more equal than others, and the little pigs—if they were properly respectful—would always roll over for the big pigs.

But the best-laid plans of mice and livestock gang aft a-gley, and the Sumo Association, bless their hearts, does not enforce the Confucian code at all costs. When a yokozuna can't win anymore, or an upstart like Asahifuji beats a brutal schedule and refuses to lose, so be it. Management endorses the Darwinian change, and institutionalizes a new Elite.

However, although sumo's elders can never entirely control the outcome of basho and the changing of the guard, they can at least plant, in the minds of sumo followers, the presumption that a basho with a disorderly script and a gang of unruly underdogs is a "bad" basho, a naughty basho, a basho after which a dignified adult can only shake his finger at the miscreants, whisper a few words of admonishment and hasten to the next—hopefully more decorous—assembly of the faithful.

This narrow view of "good basho/bad basho" curiously denies the delicate rhythm that the Sumo Association has so beautifully devised. The sumo schedule's thoughtful division into several distinct levels of difficulty and competition is wonderfully effective. Although, logically, only a few rikishi can possibly contend for the championship, the Sumo

Association's many-tiered schedule unveils an as-cending series of small dramas. At a dozen different steps along the way, small championships are won and lost. The rise of a rookie makuuchi, undersized and overeager, from the Border Patrol to the Fish Tank can be more stirring and dramatic than the battle for the yusho between the same old faces at the top. That story alone—for a real fan—can make this a good basho. There is so much happening in a basho that you can find fun almost anywhere you look. With forty wrestlers to choose from—just in makuuchi—you have forty candidates for Hero and Villain. An infinite array of possibilities—most predictable, some surprising and at least once every basho, something totally preposterous.

Good basho? Bad basho? No such thing—not if you're a real fan, not if you watch all of it, from top to bottom. Every banzuke is a different band, every basho a different melody. The schedule is always there, steady and subtle, insinuating structure on improvisation—like Curly Russell thrumming the bass in back while the Bird wails out front.

Once you've learned how to boogie, all you need is the beat.

TANK THIS ONE
for the Gipper

They cheat, you know—sumo wrestlers.

Not, however, in the same style or with the same motives as most Western sports fans recognize. Not in the tawdry, slinking, moneygrubbing style that we associate with the Black Sox of 1919 and Howard Spira of 1990. Rikishi cheat—in a way—honorably, and so, with the knowledge—nay, sanction—nay, example—of their sport's administrators.

This is a thorny concept for a foreign fan to grasp—especially one who, like me, spent a seemingly endless period of his newspaper career rooting out petty corruption among the public officials of a small town in New England. For me, it became virtually second nature, at the faintest whiff of fishy goings-on, to spring to my feet and shout, "ExCUSE me, Mr. Chairman! I believe there is Conflict of Interest here!"

Like most Americans, I'm hung up on the notion of the "public trust," a doctrine that has spawned a vast brood of commissions, institutions, volunteer ombudsmen and watchdog organizations solely dedicated to the exposure and rooting out of public officials caught in conflict of (or the "appearance of conflict of") interest. Never mind that the ones who actually get nailed are usually smalltimers and subordinates, or the occasional bigtime amateur (like Neil Bush). The system is pervasive. The fear of investigation clings democratically to all officeholders, dogging their heels as they struggle from the hustings to the bigtime. The threat is genuine, because almost anybody with a little inside information and a copy of the Law—including the unwashed nabobs of the press—can shout "conflict of interest" and raise an unholy, career-threatening stink.

Japan, on the other hand—blessed with perhaps the world's most pampered and docile press corps— has yet to discover the notion of conflict of interest. Japan is a nation in which, piously and sincerely, the individual who is interrupted in the midst of clawing, grasping, conniving, raping, and cheating his bloodstained way to personal advancement, can insist that he is acting for the greater good of all his colleagues—even his competitors—without fear that any eavesdropping buttinsky might utter even a syllable of contradiction. I note this in spite of several recent cases in Japan, in which apparent "conflicts of interest" escalated into "scandals." There was the massive insider trading scam (ca. 1988) engineered by the chairman of a company called Recruit, in which almost every power broker in Japan's ruling Liberal Democratic Party (LDP) was up to his nipples in sleaze. This was indeed revealed by the domestic press, and laboriously exposed in more than six months of nationwide publicity—which was, in turn, regarded with approbation by the international press.

Was the Recruit scandal a sign that Japan has joined the faith in regard to conflict of interest? Hardly, because the investigators from the Ministry of Justice were all LDP cohorts, with connections to the accused politicians. None of these cozy relationships were ever discussed in the English or Japanese press. When the Justice Ministry announced the indictments of several scapegoats (none of whom were influential in the LDP) and declared the investigation finished and unnewsworthy, the compliant members of the Japanese media—who depend on the LDP and the government ministries for access (and hence for their comfortable salaries and chauffeured limousines)—promptly aborted their curiosity about Recruit and set about the smelly but necessary task of rehabilitating the LDP hacks who'd been tainted (unjustly as it turns out) by the brush of scandal.

Sumo works the same way—except better. The collusion that permeates and literally governs the sumo world is more deeply intertwined, and more obvious—once you realize it's there—than in almost any other institution in Japan. And it's silly to call it a "conflict of interest" because the system encounters no conflict. It has never been criticized. In fact, it has never been acknowledged.

It's there, right under your nose, but it isn't.

Little Spoon, Tamaryu, and the Politics of Mono-ii

If, for instance, the Sumo Association were to recognize such an idea as "conflict of interest," it would have to disqualify many of its ring judges. The ring judges are oyakata—coaches—and they sit in judgment on their own wrestlers. I was pretty slow to perceive the apparent incestuousness of the judging system until the emergence in 1989 of the most popular brother act in sumo history. Takahanada (Little Spoon) in 1989 became the youngest rikishi, at seventeen, to gain promotion to juryo (the second division). A few basho later, both he and his older brother, Wakahanada (Big Spoon), were in juryo. And in a few months, Little Spoon, who was lean, long-legged, strong, handsome, reticent (sumo's first teen idol), became the youngest rikishi ever to enter makuuchi, as maegashira No. 14 in the 1990 Spring Basho. Never mind that he lost eleven times and stumbled back down to juryo. He had made history, and rejuvenated sumo. The kid had sex appeal! The musty old Sumo Association suddenly had celebrities—the hip, young, trendy kind—fighting for space in *Flash*, *Focus*, and *Friday* (Japan's versions of *People* and *Us*) with rock groups, recluses, serial killers and porn stars!

Adding poignancy to the story of Little Spoon and Big Spoon was that they were the sons of a revered oyakata, Fujishima, a former sekitori who had become—since his retirement and his emergence as a superb sumo coach—an exalted Sumo Association dignitary. The fact that Fujishima's bouncing baby boys were competent wrestlers owed to his coaching; the blinding speed of their promotion up the ranks, however, was, well, a curious coincidence. And so what if their uncle, Fujishima's father-in-law, happened to be Futagoyama, President of the Sumo Association?

So, anyway, there I was, one day, watching the juryo matches, and up onto the dohyo steps Little Spoon. And then the NHK camera swings to Fujishima, sitting there beside the ring, judging the match. His son's match. Judging his son's match, along with all his other buddies in the Sumo Association.

And I flashed back to my New England past. "Just a goddamn minute!" I shouted at the implacable television screen. "Mr. Chairman, I'm afraid Mr. Fujishima might be involved in a conflict of interest here!"

The reaction I got, sitting with a TV in an empty room, was less than gratifying.

Little Spoon and Tamaryu (his opponent) went ahead despite my protest, and fought a tenacious see-saw match, which ended dramatically as they tumbled off the dohyo together. The referee flashed his goombai, hesitantly, in Tamaryu's favor.

Not a smart move, because instantly one of the ring judges—tactfully, not Dad himself—raised a hand, challenging the ref's call and forcing a mono-ii confab in the middle of the ring. Meanwhile, NHK ran back replays of the match. No matter how you looked at it, the damn thing was a toss-up. Tamaryu had been the aggressor throughout, but Takahanada, a stronger athlete who was a good student of his father's brilliant defensive tactics, had countered and neutralized every one of Tamaryu's assaults. At the end, Tamaryu backed Takahanada to the tawara and wrenched the younger wrestler powerfully toward the seats. As Little Spoon fell, he twisted and pulled Tamaryu with him. They both plummeted off the dohyo, landing at the same instant in a violent heap.

NHK replayed the match three or four times, stopping the tape at the split second when both rikishi hit the deck. Meanwhile, the ring judges, Dad and his buddies, chewed the fat in the middle of the ring. Theoretically, they had two simple criteria to help them decide.

The first, the most important measurement, is the ring itself. If any part of a rikishi's body touches the sand outside the ring, the match is over. The first wrestler who touches, loses.

However, it is possible to amend this consideration. When both rikishi touch outside at the same time, a wrestler who has executed a strong offensive move might still be declared the winner by virtue of his initiative. Once or twice, I've seen this judgment decided in a rikishi's favor even after his foot, or a shoulder, appeared—by a fraction of a second, to have hit the dirt first.

If neither of these measurements are clear to the ring judges—after consulting, looking at marks in the sand, and reviewing the replay—they have the option of ordering an immediate re-match. This is a good face-saver for everyone.

These were the options available to the ring judges in deciding the victor in a meaningless second-division match between Takahanada and Tamaryu.

The first measurement, who touched first, was not applicable, because they'd hit the ground together. No advantage.

The second criterion fell slightly in Tamaryu's favor, because he had attacked—although indecisively—throughout the match. Advantage Tamaryu.

Still, it seemed too close to call. Why not give everyone a graceful compromise and have them wrestle again? Sorry. Life is not so simple.

When ring judges get together for mono ii, they have more matters to consider than merely which of these pugs dragged his piggies across the tawara first. In the back of their minds, they must also weigh, for example,

• The relative importance of the two sumobeya involved.

In this case, Little Spoon, from Fujishima-beya, was a veritable prince among rikishi, one of a team of rising Fujishima pupils who would eventually supplant Kokonoe-beya as sumo's showcase stable. Tamaryu, on the other hand, comes from Katanami-beya, a weak house with little influence and no prospects. Advantage Takahanada.

• The relative prestige of the two rikishi involved. Little Spoon was programmed for stardom, his recognition factor already comparable to Chiyonofuji, Konishiki and Buddha. Moreover, he was the keystone of the Sumo Association's efforts to regain the interest of Japan's fickle youth. When he set foot on the dohyo, a great feminine cheer went up in the arena. He was, simply, the most watched, most liked, most hoped-for wrestler in sumo. Tamaryu, on the other hand, was an old journeyman who was gradually slipping toward retirement. He labored in obscurity, destined for oblivion. His value to the prestige and the future of the Sumo Association was, exactly, zero. Advantage Takahanada.

• The composition of the panel of judges. Fujishima, Little Spoon's father and oyakata, was one of the judges. Katanami, Tamaryu's oyakata, was not. Advantage Takahanada.

• Previous debts and obligations among all the parties involved. Without knowing all the byzantine connections that link the sumo world, it's impossible to determine who owed what to whom among the group that included Little Spoon and Tamaryu, Fujishima and Katanami, and all the judges on the dohyo. It would be safe to assume that Fujishima, whose position and wealth are near the pinnacle of the Sumo Association, held more markers than Tamaryu and his lowly coach. Advantage Takahanada.

It's possible to infer a number of other transactional factors into the conference that determined the outcome of that match between Takahanada and Tamaryu. But the result would be the same: advantage Takahanada. In the underworld of business and politics with which I grew so familiar in the West, the issue was cut and dried. Regardless of how well or badly he might have performed—once the decision was ripped from the ref's hands— Takahanada had this victory in the bag.

A Sense of Honor

But there's more.

Within that little circle of pompous men in black robes, there was still another dynamic working. They were groping, in a few minutes of quiet intercourse, for something that sumo people call *rei*. You can translate the word differently according to the context, so that it comes out as "propriety," "order," "dignity," "politeness," "respect," or "balance." You can even define it as "class" or "the right stuff." In this case, the definition might be closer to "fairness," or even closer: "honor."

The quality that these five cloistered and mildly paranoid sumo judges held in common—which would be well-nigh impossible to find among any group of five corporate executives in any nation, including Japan—is a sense of honor. With that quality present, Tamaryu claimed at least one additional shred of advantage.

This "sense of honor" stuff sounds noble, and I think it's really there—fighting it out with baser instincts in the hearts of the sumo elders—on every close call. But balance that wishful inference with the fact that every mono ii conference that ever occurred, like discussions among NFL officials after a disputed touchdown, is an impenetrable secret. You may impute motives (nice or nasty) to these old guys, but you can't verify them. The sense that emerges from sumo insiders about the context of these meetings is that ring judges exercise a strange blend of deep myopia and extreme farsightedness.

In the near view, the ring judges focus on the events of this particular match at this moment. Regardless of the potential embarrassment to a member of their panel, or to Sumo Association's hierarchy, they will not reverse a decision in which there is clear physical (a toe-print on the sand) or visual (NHK's replay) evidence to the contrary.

Between this narrow plane of physical evidence and a distant peak that might be termed "the best interests of sumo," the ring judges don't see very much. It just isn't important to these guys how their decision affects the record of Takahanada or

Tamaryu in this basho. It isn't even important whether fans or sportswriters see their decision as fair, whether Fujishima's presence as a judge for his own son's match might look fishy to an outsider.

The fan is expected to believe that these judges are perfectly impartial because they mean to be impartial—as a matter of honor. The fan must believe—despite all evidence to the contrary—that what appears at the moment to be cheating will actually become, in the long run, a profound justice, a sort of transcendent fairness. Strip the judges, the sport, of this necessary suspension of disbelief, and you discredit sumo irreparably. Impose onto sumo the temporal concept of conflict of interest, and you take away the strange confusion of values—sports and religion—that makes sumo so much fun for even those who don't know a rugby ball from a catcher's mask.

You must, despite the urge to scoff, embrace the dubious assertion that on the rare occasions when ring judges interfere with the outcome of a match and change it without any apparent regard for fairness, they perceive a higher morality. They're shining their rei on the masses.

For instance, the ring judges—Dad and the boys—decided the match in favor of Takahanada. Tamaryu, the apparent winner, bowed stoically and made his exit. He had had a sweet victory in his grasp. He was an old poop on his last legs but—until they snatched it away from him—he'd kicked sand on the rich kid and felt some of the old bounce seep back into his step. When they told Tamaryu, "No, you can't have this one," he took it like a man. Tamaryu's loss was an injustice in the short term. But in the long term, we fans are advised to recognize a defeat that served Tamaryu and Katanami far better than an impertinent victory would have. Perhaps the ring judges realized that, in claiming a disputed victory over Little Spoon and thus slowing the rich kid's inevitable progress to the upper ranks, Tamaryu would suffer a small measure of disfavor from Uncle Futagoyama and other powerful members of the Sumo Association. Tamaryu was close to retirement; he was in line, perhaps, to take over management of a sumobeya—an expensive and difficult undertaking that requires financial aid and political favor within the Sumo Association. Any resentment that fell to Tamaryu would damage his prospects. It would also affect his oyakata, Katanami, and their small, impecunious sumobeya.

Consider, on the other hand, the blessings to Tamaryu as he bowed graciously to an unjust defeat. There was the gratitude of the Sumo Association, who could herald yet another victory for the nation's most popular sports star. There was an obligation, a favor owed to Tamaryu and Katanami by Fujishima, a giant in the sumo world. And there was the unspoken sympathy of all those who knew that Tamaryu accepted a humiliating reversal without a peep of complaint—with class. Rei!

"Yaocho Doesn't Exist"

Call it cheating or conflict of interest, the occasional tampering of the ring judges (in essence, the Sumo Association itself) sets a tone for the sport of sumo. The message conveyed is that, as long as motives remain "pure" and directed toward the preservation of order, certain results are negotiable.

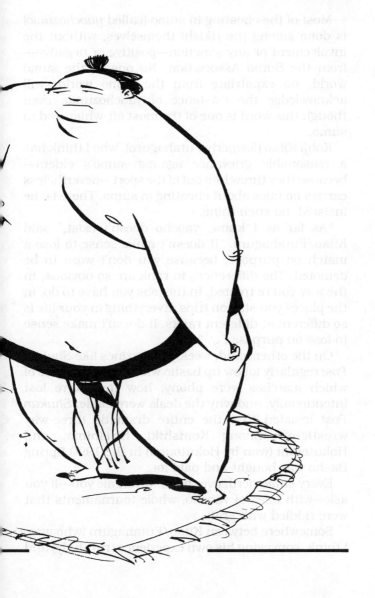

Most of the cheating in sumo (called yaocho[zumo]) is done among the rikishi themselves, without the involvement of any outsiders—positively in public— ... from the Sumo Association. No one in the sumo world, no expatriate from that ... ... acknowledge the ... chance of ... ... though the word is one of the most off- ... to sumo.

Kohji ... ... who I think has a reasonable grievance against sumo's estab- ... because they threw him out of the sport—never ... carries no taboo about cheating in sumo. There's, he ... instead no such thing.

"As far as I know, yaocho [isn't illegal]," said Kitao/Futabayama. "It doesn't make sense to lose a match on purpose, because you don't want to be demoted. The difference in rank can be so obvious, in the way you're treated. In the jobs you have to do, in the places you sit on trips, everything in your life is so different on different ranks. It doesn't make sense to lose on purpose."

On the other hand, ... matches like Shukan Post regularly follow up bashou, how, many of which matches were phony, how they were lost intentionally, and only the deals worked. The Shukan Post focused on the entire division ... there were wrestlers ... ... (Kitashima) ... ... Hokutoumi (won by Hokutoumi) ... spring Basho ... Konishiki and ...

Every time ... ... decide you—if you ask—with ... ... the whole tournaments that were riddled with ...

Somewhere between ... (Futabayama) who was ... ...

Most of the cheating in sumo (called *yaochozumo*) is done among the rikishi themselves, without the involvement or any sanction—positive or negative—from the Sumo Association. No one in the sumo world, no expatriate from the sumo world, will acknowledge the existence of yaochozumo, even though this word is one of the most oft-whispered in sumo.

Kohji Kitao (formerly Futahaguro), who I think has a reasonable grievance against sumo's elders—because they threw him out of the sport—nevertheless carries no tales about cheating in sumo. There is, he insisted, no such thing.

"As far as I know, yaocho doesn't exist," said Kitao/Futahaguro. "It doesn't make sense to lose a match on purpose, because you don't want to be demoted. The differences in rank are so obvious, in the way you're treated, in the jobs you have to do, in the places you stay on trips. Everything in your life is so different at different ranks. It doesn't make sense to lose on purpose . . . "

On the other hand, weekly magazines like *Shukan Post* regularly follow up basho with expert analysis of which matches were phony, how they were lost intentionally, and why the deals were made. *Shukan Post* insisted that the entire dramatic three-way wrestle-off among Konishiki, Kirishima, and Hokutoumi (won by Hokutoumi) in the 1990 Spring Basho was bought and paid for.

Every sumo nerd, over beer, will regale you—if you ask—with tales of yaocho, whole tournaments that were riddled with graft.

Somewhere between Kitao/Futahaguro (who was, I think, conveying his own experience truthfully) and

Shukan Post (whose veracity, while not unimpeach-able, cannot be completely scorned) lies the truth about yaochozumo.

On the record, yaocho does not exist. It never happened. It never will. Every single match in the history of sumo was on the up-and-up.

Accept this and you may also accept that jockeys never hold horses back in the stretch, and that prize fighters never go into the tank in fear for their lives and their careers. Illegal substances—from barbitu-rates to steroids to human grown hormone—have been completely eradicated in track and field, weightlifting, professional football and bodybuilding. Blood doping is nonexistent in bicycle racing. College athletes never receive hundred-dollar handshakes. College basketball players never shave points.

If yaocho did exist, however, it would not enjoy the vast underworld scale of operations attributed by the weekly magazines. If yaocho did exist, it would partake of the moderation that typifies sumo—watched over and regulated by the Sumo Association. It would serve to maintain balance in sumo, reverence for rank and the proper order of things: rei.

If this were so, then it's reasonable to believe that the 1990 Spring Basho wrestle-off among Konishiki, Kirishima, and Hokutoumi might have been ar-ranged—as *Shukan Post* claimed—with the blessing of the Sumo Association. Though two rikishi lost the yusho, each gained. In succumbing to Hokutoumi, Konishiki assured himself of a lead-pipe yokozuna nomination if he dominated the next basho (he didn't). Kirishima, while losing to Hokutoumi, assured his immediate promotion to ozeki (which he received). And Hokutoumi, who struggled but won, reasserted the primacy of the Kokonoe-beya as sumo's foremost stable, while subtly indicating that he—as a rikishi—was still subordinate to Chiyonofuji, his stablemate.

It all had the lovely, Confucian symmetry that the Sumo Association so cherishes. And yet, I resist the insistence that this complicated wrestle-off was crooked—for one reason. To tamper with a series of matches so important and so public is indiscreet—a word I have yet to associate with anything the Sumo Association has ever done. If there were deals involved in that wrestle-off, they were implicit—understood well beforehand among all the rikishi, all the oyakata, all the knowing elders of the Sumo Association.

The Last-Day Blues

Hence, my suspicion—with reservations—was that the wrestle-off was legit. In fact, I think most sumo matches are legit. I once thought, with Kitao/ Futahaguro, that all sumo matches were legit. This belief persisted through five or six basho, until I grew vaguely uneasy with the dullness that seemed to grip the basho on the day—Day 15—when it should be most exciting. This is a big day not just because the Elite are deciding the title, but because another six, eight, ten rikishi, all up and down the banzuke, are sweating out kachikoshi.

In any basho, there are rikishi who get through fourteen days of wrestling at seven wins and seven losses. In order to make kachikoshi, 8–7, and fend off demotion, they have to win that last match. Often, they have to do it against higher-ranked rikishi. Often, they have to overcome losing streaks, poor health, injuries and ennui. They must summon all their grit and skill, go out in the dirt weary and woozy, and bust a gut just one more time.

So why, I said to myself after watching four or five Day 15s, are these last-gasp kachikoshi matches so sloppy, short and desultory? Fatsoyama doesn't seem to care. Kitao said that demotion is the rikishi's greatest fear. So why did these matches seem to lack any sense of desperation?

I began to form an answer to these questions when I began to notice that rikishi who come to Day 15 at 7–7 almost never lose. I figured I'd better find out for sure, so I started keeping count. Between January '89 and July '90, there were 56 Day 15 matches that involved wrestlers who were 7–7 before the match. Thanks to careful scheduling by the Sumo Association, only eight of those matches involved rikishi who were both 7–7, therefore dooming one of them to certain makekoshi. The scarcity of head-to-heads between 7–7 rikishi isn't accidental. When one of the two rikishi has no chance for kachikoshi—sumo's version of sudden death—it's not good management (although it's fun!).

I removed those eight head-to-heads from my statistics, and found that the kachikoshi rate for rikishi entering Day 15 at 7–7 was 39 wins, nine losses—a winning percentage of .813.

Now, it didn't make sense that a bunch of guys who'd gone through two weeks of win-one/lose-one sumo could suddenly boost themselves to a championship level of performance—even though motivated by desperation. Sixty percent, perhaps 67 percent, was believable. Eighty percent was Neverneverland— especially in light of the fact that 21 of these victories, more than half, came against equal or higher-ranked opponents.

Even more convincing than these statistics was the eyewitness evidence. I was watching lousy sumo. The winners in these desperate matches were blasé, the losers were sluggish and then—it seemed— embarrassed, hurrying to get away.

Kitao/Futahaguro was right. A rikishi will resist demotion at almost any cost. Fortunately, the cost isn't high and help is abundant. A rikishi in danger of makekoshi near the end of a basho often finds that his schedule has gotten easier.

But the schedule is still a risk. According to the unsubstantiated gossip that has circulated among sumo observers for decades, yaochozumo begins with two sumobeya flunkies, silently empowered to negotiate on behalf of two rikishi who are scheduled to wrestle one another. One rikishi needs a win. The other is off the bubble; either he has kachikoshi already, or he's already taken his eighth loss and can't be salvaged. Either way, he has a favor to give.

The two elves exchange pleasantries and discuss terms. No one in sumo—not the Sumo Association, not their oyakata, not even the two rikishi them-selves—is ever informed of what transpires between the two elves. The rikishi are aware, however, that the meeting occurred, and that an obligation was incurred.

How to Take a Dive

The next day, in the consummation of that wordless contract, the voluntary loser applies one of several techniques to his own defeat.

If he's inexperienced at taking a dive, there is some

danger that he could accidentally win—causing embarrassment to his sumobeya and incurring an obligation, for atonement, severalfold greater than the original deal. Hence, the safest method for the yaocho novice is, literally, to take a dive: hataki komi, the matador. It's easy. At the moment of tachiai, the designated "loser" charges slightly crooked at the designated "winner." The winner anticipates this clue and deftly sidesteps the loser's misguided launch. He taps the loser up-side the head, thumps him on the back and guides him into the dirt. Easy as rolling off a log.

The matador occurs with extraordinary frequency on Day 15.

For a slightly more sophisticated yaocho, the "salami squeeze" is popular—because it's not quite as obvious as the matador. When executing the salami squeeze, the designated "winner" allows the designated "loser" to achieve morozashi—both arms inside. The cleverness of this tactic is that, even though the loser has dominant hand position, he wastes it. His hands, pathetically, seem to forget their function, and suddenly there he is, backpedaling helplessly. He looks like a man trying—to no avail—to lift an immense, uncooperative sausage. He pauses momentarily at the tawara, hugging the winner, groping at his back, reaching impotently for a mawashi that he just can't seem to find. "Goddammit, where is that belt?! Oops. Too late . . . "

He's out. Match over. Another kachikoshi.

My favorite form of yaocho is "dirty dancing." Sumo's handful of great dirty dancers are so artful that they have restored much of my appreciation of Day 15. Dirty dancers are oldtimers, Butterballs and

Cabdrivers mostly, who bounce up and down the Fish Tank, doing each other favors.

Dirty dancing looks like a real match. The designated "loser" seizes a slight advantage at tachiai, and then applies his best technique, his strongest move—and he's got it! He won! Oh no, not quite. Just missed!

They repeat this charade several times. The loser gets the winner in trouble, and then they strain, they grunt. At the last second, ever so subtly, the loser relaxes. The winner escapes the loser's grip just far enough to avert defeat. Finally, as the dance nears its end, the loser executes an almost perfect throw. Almost! He misses by a millimeter, and then—alas—having committed himself, he's off-balance, vulnerable . . . whap! . . . and down.

When it's over, and you watch the NHK replay, and if you watch intelligently, you begin to see that the loser never really used his advantage and the winner was never in danger. They have performed an artful illusion. Bruno Sammartino and Hulk Hogan couldn't've pulled it off any prettier.

The Rite of Passage

When I began to watch these questionable sumo matches, applying my senses, skepticism and statistics, I was upset with sumo—for allowing this flagrant deception, for fooling me. I don't like to be taken for a sucker. On reflection, however, my outrage withered.

I soothed myself with the perverse consolation that almost every sport we know and love not only contains cheating but—like the Sumo Association looking away from those wheeler-dealer flunkies—

tolerates it. Drugs, scams, point-shaving, gambling, prejudiced judges—they're everywhere. Heck, Knute, they took steroids at Notre Dame!

I feel more consoled, however, by my awareness of yaochozumo's context and limitations. I know almost every match in which it is likely to occur. I know that it is largely confined to the maegashira ranks and to the attainment of kachikoshi, by any means possible. I know that virtually 90 percent of all yaocho occurs within the last three days of a basho, with most of that action on Day 15. Even in a basho riddled with yaocho, I have spotted, at most, ten phony matches—in a total of at least 280. And I've even come to take a perverse enjoyment in inviting friends to watch Day 15—so I can predict the results (with uncanny accuracy) of certain matches. I keep thinking of the joke about the moron (choose your ethnic group) who lost a week's wages betting on instant replay.

As I've pondered yaocho, also, I've developed a grudging admiration for the Sumo Association's almost mystical power to oversee it without seeing it. Sumo's elders keep their little cheating problem in check first by the skillful use of the schedule, giving rikishi every chance to avoid a last-day crisis. Extending this sense of control beyond one basho, I've noticed that yaochozumo follows a kind of ebb and flow, proliferating for a while, until some silent signal from the Sumo Association curtails it abruptly.

It appears—and Kitao/Futahaguro's disavowal supports the supposition—that many young rikishi are weaned gradually (perhaps reluctantly) into the ways of yaocho. The secret is kept away from those (like Futahaguro) who don't need help, from those who wouldn't benefit enough from it, and especially from those who might be indiscreet. By allowing it but holding the secret tightly within a chosen brotherhood, sumo's elders control yaocho more effectively than if they tried to ban it.

Yaocho's profoundest hold on rikishi—and the reason, I think, that the secret is so well guarded—lies in its use as a rite of passage into sumo's inner circle.

As he reflected on his ten years in sumo, one of Kitao/Futahaguro's most heartfelt remarks was this: "The rikishi bow to each other before the match and after. Sumo people say that sumo begins with politeness and ends with politeness. That's a beautiful tradition, one of the things I miss most of all."

Naturally, in saying this, Kitao/Futahaguro used the word "rei," for "politeness."

Eventually, in that spirit of "beginning with politeness," each rikishi, at some point, is initiated into sumo's secret brotherhood by accepting sport's politest offer. What higher act of rei than to concede the victory to an opponent who needs it? And what better sign of rei in the initiate than the gracious acceptance of the offer? And what better test of a rikishi's commitment to the brotherhood than his willingness to subordinate his competitive passion to the greater good of all, the collective need? Especially when he knows that he won't get in trouble for it! And even better that he knows it will help break down those icy walls that stand between sumobeya, and will make him feel—once and for all—like one of the guys!

Yaocho prevents great upheavals in the ranks, and makes change a gentle process. All the new blood is filtered and diluted by the humbling process of yaocho. One of the sumo nuances that the observant fan eventually perceives is that a young rikishi proves his readiness to compete at the highest level not by showing that he can win in makuuchi, but by developing a talent for judicious defeat.

Thus, yaocho also identifies dissenters, those whose pride inhibits them from losing even a meaningless match, even to help a colleague. Those rikishi aren't cast out indiscreetly (perhaps for fear that they might speak up), but their path becomes harder, their progress slower, their status always a little shaky. Among the most prominent of these uneasy princes are Onokuni and Asahifuji. If they have submitted to yaocho, they didn't do it often enough or with the proper alacrity. Some rikishi, I think—especially former collegiate wrestlers—are never initiated into the yaocho club at all, because they might not be trustworthy. Sumo gets them too late in life, too fully formed and ethically fastidious.

As they govern all other aspects of their sport, sumo's elders govern yaocho with a politeness that borders on intimidation. No one, even a yaocho resister, ever steps very far out of line. To betray the group is tantamount to betraying one's family. When a rikishi resorts to yaocho, he will use it sparingly, silently, with dignity (rei), and with a consciousness that yaocho serves to keep the family in balance.

Yaocho is an invisible, but palpable presence in sumo. Look for it, and you'll never spot it. Even its resisters—and I'm certain there are some—will deny its existence. By comparison, the Cheshire Cat's smile is a bite on the ass. But yaocho works powerfully and consistently—counteracting one of sumo's greatest problems, the loneliness and persistent mediocrity of most rikishi—stuck forever in the maegashira and juryo ranks. It keeps giving new life to those whose hopes have waned, to the working stiffs of sumo. When someone takes a dive on your behalf, it keeps you afloat. When you tank a match for another guy, you feel a little more deeply the sympathy of your group, your sense of belonging. You can win all alone, but cheating needs company.

Look at it this way. If Jake LaMotta had learned how to take a decent dive, Vicki might've stuck with him, and *Raging Bull* might've had a happy ending.

THE STATISTICAL IMPERATIVE

Statistics are the lifeblood of sports.

To make the metaphor more apt, I should say that sports burn human energy like forests inhale carbon dioxide, and spew out stats the way the leaves excrete oxygen.

One reason why sumo's prestige as a sport is so tenuous: it has a stats gap. This explains why sumo, as a regular diet, is difficult for many serious fans to digest, and why it does not capture the initiate, the child, the hermit, the sideline lip-gnawer or the gamesman with the same spontaneity—even obsessiveness—that occurs with baseball or golf, soccer or the NFL. The action, the game itself, lures many fans, but there's a different sort of fan who needs statistics more than the fleeting flashes of human struggle, the sort of fan (well, nut) who feels torn between love of the games and fascination for the wondrous, endless possibilities for trivial bookkeeping that throb within the games.

Florence Nightingale, reportedly a Washington Senators fan, once said, "To understand God's purpose, we must study statistics, for these are the measure of his purpose."

On the other hand, Scotty Bowman, possibly also with the Senators in mind, retorted, "Statistics are for losers."

The balance is, simply, that statistics help illuminate the game. Even sumo nerds have sensed this and tried to fill the stats gap. Instinctively, these interpreters of sumo's mystic meaning have used history as their portal to enlightenment, dragging readers into museums to look at *engishiki* dolls and into libraries to ponder mildewed passages in the *Nihongi.* Such studies tend to confirm an impression that sumo's history is vague and quaint, because vagueness and quaintness—read "cultural differences"—are precisely what feeds this viewpoint. All of sumo's rituals—though explained in relentless detail and with glowering earnestness—come off as Shinto charades, imitations of some greater, deeper, more fearful rite within the imponderable psyche of Japan. But where's the Game in all this? This esoterica sends no message to the fan because it comes without superlatives—the Most, the Longest, Shortest, Quickest, Highest Total . . .

There ain't enough numbers. Let's face it, Howard. You can't really compare Tsunenohana (1910–30) to Taiho (1956–71) to Chiyonofuji (1970–91), not the way you can compare Ruth to DiMaggio to Aaron to Oh. Or Baugh to Bradshaw to Montana. Which means you can't work up a decent full-scale, table-thumping, "All right, asshole, let's look it UP!" barroom argument.

The Data Deficit

The main statistic in sumo is each rikishi's won/lost record—a rather dismal number in itself since two-thirds of all rikishi end their careers below .500.

As a pale facsimile of stats, sumo information also provides such items as height and weight, and the guy's hometown ("Folks, here's an interesting stat! Since 1750, Fatsoyama is only the third rikishi to make it to makuuchi from the town of West Tokushima!"). The pre-basho info kit also tells the stat-hungry fan how many yusho (usually none) each rikishi has won, how many Fighting Spirit, Technique and Outstanding Wrestler prizes he's won instead of the yusho, how old he was (usually fifteen) when he entered sumo, how old when he was promoted to the upper divisions, what his rank was in the last basho, and, of course, the name of his sumobeya. Obviously, this is more of a résumé than a statistical profile.

During the matches, occasionally, a commentator will reel off some fascinating statistical tidbit—perhaps noting that at age 31, Kirishima was the sixth (or fifth, or seventh—whatever) oldest rikishi in history to gain promotion to ozeki.

Terrific, but answer me this: what's his batting average in the clutch?

What were his splits?

What was his hang time?

Now I'm not a stats freak. Nope. What I represent— as anyone can plainly see—is a healthy, mainstream interest in sports numbers. I am one of millions who believe you can't enjoy sports fully without you got stats. So I asked myself how could I introduce new and useful numbers to the numberless wasteland of sumo? The answer, which came to me in a kind of self-illuminating Siddharthan literary epiphany, was fiendishly simple!

Rating the Rikishi

It's obvious to anyone who contemplates the notion of introducing new statistical measurements to the sport of sumo that no such innovation would earn the blessing of the Sumo Association. However, in order to enlist support from even one of sumo's multitude of less official guardians, any new statistics must still recognize and incorporate the Sumo Association's rankings. Bearing this in mind, I said: "Why not assign a numerical value to all the rikishi in sumo's upper division, and why not make those values parallel to the rankings established every two months in the Sumo Association's banzuke?"

So I did.

My rikishi rating (RR) system gives points, from 1 to 20, to each rikishi, according to his place on the official pecking order. The maximum, 20 points, goes only to yokozuna who are at the very pinnacle of the sumo world. The lowest rating applies to the bottom of the Fish Tank, the Border Patrol and to juryo wrestlers who receive one-day invitations to compete in makuuchi.

The rating system, as I've applied it to the day-today competition in each basho since January, 1989, breaks down in the following order.

YOKOZUNA: 16–20 points

As you might guess, the only yokozuna who has ever enjoyed an RR of 20 was Chiyonofuji. This happened twice, and he only earned it after he had won two straight yusho and had been undefeated in the previous basho. Under less brilliant conditions, a yokozuna who wins tournaments, or contends consistently, is worth 18–19 points. Gravy Train yokozuna are worth only 17 points and can sink as low as 16.

OZEKI: 15–17 points

The rule of thumb for yokozuna applies to ozeki wrestlers. A steady contender deserves 17 points. An ozeki coming off a bad basho is worth 16 points. An ozeki who's permanently resigned to the Gravy Train deserves only 15 points.

SEKIWAKE: 11–16 points

Occasionally, a sekiwake emerges before the basho as an ozeki candidate and a genuine yusho contender—as Kirishima did in the 1990 Summer Basho. In that rare case, you have a 16-point sekiwake. Sekiwake who aren't really in the running for advancement, but are keeping a grip on the Tightrope from basho to basho—as Kotogaume and Sakahoko did for many months—are bonafide 15-pointers. New sekiwake, up from komusubi, are worth 12–14 points, depending on their chances. On the rare occasion when a Cannon Fodder competitor gets a battlefield promotion from maegashira all the day competition in each league since January, 1960. It breaks down in the following order:

YOKOZUNA: 16-20 points

As you might guess, the only Yokozuna who has ever enjoyed an HR of 20 was Chiyonofuji. This happened twice, and he only earned it after he had won two straight basho and had been undefeated in the previous basho. Under less brilliant conditions a Yokozuna with nine tournaments ... of ... consists ... ... later ... is worth 18-19 points. Every train ... trains are worth only 17 points and can work as

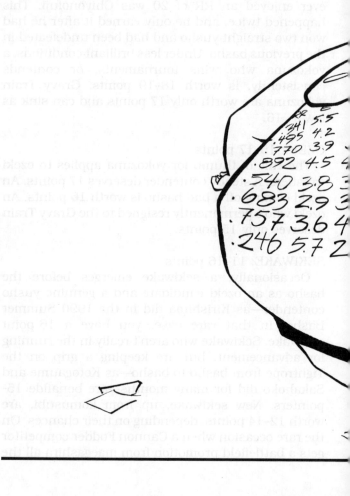

341 5.5
.495 4.2
.770 3.9
.892 4.5 4
.540 3.8 3
.683 2.9 3
.757 3.6 4
.246 5.7 2

... 17 points

... time of volcanic ... applies to each ... number deserves 17 points. An ... trainee is worth 16 points. An ... results resigned to the Grey Train ... 15 points.

KOMAWARE: 11-16 points

Occasionally a sekiwake emerges before the basho as an ... contender and a perfect wa to contender. As Kirishima did in the 1990 Summer basho ... that rare case ... you have a 16 point ... sake. Sekiwake who aren't really in the running for advancement but are keeping a grip on the ... rank ... from basho to basho—as Kotogame and Sakahoko did for some months before both 15-pointers. New sekiwake, anyway improbable, are worth 12-14 points depending on their chances. On the rare occasion when a Cannon Fodder competitor gets a bald field promotion from one ... to all the

way to sekiwake, without stopping in the Meatgrinder, the reasonable expectation is that he will be annihilated and sent back down. Hence, the appropriate rating is 11 or 12.

KOMUSUBI: 10 points
Komusubi is a plateau. The two guys in the Meatgrinder are always rated at 10 points.

MAEGASHIRA: 1–9 points
In assigning points to the rank-and-file rikishi, I usually follow a logical sequence of giving the maximum to one or two guys on top of the Cannon Fodder squad and then reducing the rating at regular intervals all the way down. However, I adjust this according to my assessment of the rikishi whom the Sumo Association has—sometimes willy-nilly—placed at these levels.

For instance, in the 1989 Summer Basho, I rated the East maegashira No. 1, Daijuyama, at only 8 points, because I regarded him as a weak representative in that position. His final record was 4–11. Two basho later, in the 1989 Autumn Basho, I gave all three of the top-rated maegashira—Kirishima, Mitoizumi and Akinoshima—the maximum 9 points, because they were the best three rikishi to occupy those positions in many moons. Together, despite the crippling pressure of the Cannon Fodder schedule, they compiled a 24–21 record, and beat the Elite seven times.

In practice, these numerical ratings—which are directly parallel to the Sumo Association's assessment of the wrestlers' competitive strength—become scores. When a rikishi wins, he tallies (on the

Benjamin scorecard) points equal to his opponent's rikishi rating (RR). For instance, beat one of the two komusubi, and you get 10 points.

The loser, on the other hand, scores nothing.

Over the course of the fifteen days of competition, what happens is the ideal consummation of every sport: a score!

For example, in the New Year Basho of 1991, Kirishima had a 14–1 record, won the championship and scored 140 points, compared to runner-up Hokutoumi, with a 12–3 record and 117 points. Everybody had a score, all the way down to Tagaryu, who was 5–10 with nine (9) points.

The virtues of scoring lie not only in such obvious benefits as How Much a rikishi scored, but also in How Much he Coulda scored. With scores, a myriad variety of comparisons begin to develop. For example, in that same basho, Kirishima's only loss was to Akinoshima, who was komusubi (10 points)—which means Kirishima Coulda scored 150 points. By comparison, Hokutoumi (117 points, remember?) Coulda scored 159 points, and old Tagaryu (nine points) down there Coulda managed a mere 26 points if he'd won every match—which shows how weak his schedule was (and he still couldn't win!).

You see, a scoring system helps compare schedules. The difference between Hokutoumi's 159-point schedule and Tagaryu's 26-point schedule demonstrates graphically the immense gap between the Elite in sumo and the guys in the Fish Tank.

Furthermore, by maintaining a day-to-day scoresheet during a basho (which I do), the fan has an additional touchstone for the drama of competition. In the first week of a basho, it's possible for a

Fish Tank rikishi to go undefeated and stand side-by-side, in won-lost record, with the mightiest yokozuna. But point totals, reflecting the quality of opponents, show the phenomenal fish in his true light—way down in the standings where he belongs.

Beyond the individual tournament, the faithful sumo statistician—using the Benjamin system—inevitably accumulates data that compare rikishi, as competitors, over the long term. Among the stats I've created to compare rikishi scientifically, not only in one basho but over many basho, the most important are as follows:

OAR (Opponents' Average Rating). By averaging the values of all Fatsoyama's opponents, we know precisely how tough his schedule really is. For the year 1989, Asahifuji's and Hokutenyu had some of sumo's toughest schedules, with an OAR of 11.7. The easiest ride was for Kitakachidoki, whose OAR was only 2.8.

APM (Average Points per Match). By dividing the numbers of points by the number of matches, we see—at a glance—the strength and consistency of a rikishi's performance, day in and day out. Chiyonofuji, the best in 1989, had an APM of 9.38. Asahifuji, with a tougher schedule, managed only 7.74. Toyonoumi, the worst, scored just 2.36 points per match.

APB (Average Points per Basho). By extending this simple statistic back through four basho, the statistician derives a splendid, simple device for identifying the best rikishi over that period. It is the sumo equivalent to the National Football League's quarterback ratings.

For example, in the rating period from September

1990 through March 1991, the Top Ten rated rikishi were as follows:

Rikishi	Points	Rating (APB)
1. Asahifuji	464	116.00
2. Hokutoumi	463	115.75
3. Onokuni	410	102.00
4. Chiyonofuji	396	99.00
Kotonishiki	396	99.00
6. Kirishima	379	94.75
7. Konishiki	339	84.75
8. Akinoshima	306	6.50
9. Tochinowaka	243	60.75
10. Terao	238	59.50

The system, I believe, is simple. The permutations and resulting analyses are infinite.

In trying to expand sumo's statistics, I am merely striving to show (a) that there is vast potential in this untrod field of play and (b) that it's a do-it-yourself effort. Since the official sumo folks are sure to stick to their own paltry arithmetic, the fan is a statistical entrepreneur. The numbers in this chapter represent a pittance of venture capital.

Use it or ignore it, but listen. If a bunch of you should happen to draw up a draft list and start the First Sumo Rotisserie League, I hope you'll get in touch with me, so I can play. And if one of you, alone and palely loitering in your living room with an empty bottle, a broken heart, and NHK, should happen to start up an imaginary sumo league (the Universal Sumo Association, Inc.?), well, don't forget me! Even though I've (honest to God) outgrown that sort of thing, I'd still love to see your power matrices, probability tables and stress charts, and I'd like to know whether—as your engine of chance—you decided to use dice, or playing cards, or one of those new doo-hickeys . . . you know, a computer.

13

THEIR BODIES,
OUR SELVES

Yeah, but the feel of sumo . . .

Go back to Ryogoku.

Look around the pit, full to the rafters. They're standing up against the back walls. There's excitement in the air, but . . .

Don't fall too hard. This is mostly just the normal thrill of bigtime sports and it's pretty much the same at Tiger Stadium on Bat Day. Dig deeper. The odd thing is that everyone here is so mellow. This arena is more homey and relaxed than the average Japanese home. Why all these middle-aged ladies in their Sunday best; all the rough-handed, merry old men? Why that little girl, somebody's granddaughter, climbing over a low rail and planting a bare foot in the neighbors' rice? And why all this mirth—everybody in the vicinity suddenly bursting into laughter as they pick rice from between the little girl's toes?

Tradition (or history) doesn't explain the intimacy of 11,000 people packed willingly, joyfully together in this immense sardine can. Noh dramas and ikebana exhibitions have no such power to shatter people's instinctive reserve. Culture? No—because it is axiomatic in Japanese culture that strangers forced to occupy too small a space together plunge into morose silence and treat one another like festering lepers. Nor is the charm entirely in the game itself. Some of those old men don't know one wrestler from another, and the ladies—many only pause in their chatter long enough to gape at the grand, voluptuous entrances and recessionals of the rikishi. And certainly, the allure lies not at all in stats, nor very much in strategy and tactics. Are they here for the thrill of victory and the agony of defeat? Well, partly, but . . .

Psychology? Some deep-seated need?

Spare me.

Orwell suggests that they're out for pain. "Serious sport has nothing to do with fair play. It is bound up with hatred, jealousy, boastfulness, disregard of all rules and sadistic pleasure in witnessing violence . . . "

Close maybe, but Orwell's analysis evades sumo's unparalleled imbalance between the glimpses of violence and the excruciating waltz of preparation and politesse. Better violence is so easy to come by. You could rent *Women in Love* at the corner video joint.

The magic, the secret joy of sumo for the fan is tangled up in simply being here. Staring at the men.

Being near them. Imagining the feel of them. Actually rushing up to pat them, the fat on their enormous backs clammy and squishy.

Go back.

The First Principle is The Flesh Itself.

On one of Tokyo's oppressive August days, I was on a commuter train, and an old man, small and sixtyish, got on. He looked around sullenly at the absence of available seats, then stretched an arm up to grab a strap. I began to watch him.

The old man wore a railroad workman's uniform, and the cap—reminiscent of the Imperial Army infantry—to go with it. He was bony and hungry-looking. But he reminded me of a sumo wrestler—because of the arm that held him upright.

Without thinking about it, the old man balanced against the sway and lurch of the train, hanging by that arm. Unlike a younger, or heavier man's arm, it had no natural layer of fat between skin and muscle. It was like an exposed driveshaft. It was rods and cables twining and flexing beneath a millimeter of skin. The only muscle in that spare bundle of sinew was the muscle he had used all his life, to work. It occurred to me that if you'd forced him to the floor and ordered him to do pushups, he might manage a few and then fail—because a pushup was something he never needed to do, and so the muscles best-suited for such things had just atrophied and melted away, thus saving him the effort of carrying them around. But ask him, ask those steel cables in his arm to seize, to lift, to move, carry, shift, pull, twist, release, fit, press, hold steady and wait—all those tasks the arm had performed incessantly and insensibly for fifty years on the job—and this he could do all day without rest or discomfort. Given its proper duty, that arm was unbreakable, unfrayable and tireless as a vise.

I knew this without testing the old man. I knew because of Papa, my grandfather, who did those things—seize, lift, carry, shift, twist, fit, press, hold steady—for 53 years in the Milwaukee Road frog shops. He fit and cut, repaired and welded the spiders of steel that joined rails and guided engines. His arms, though thicker, were like those of the old man on the train—the unbidden, unconsidered fruit of his labor, the homely apotheosis of the International Brotherhood of Machinists. Papa's arms—like those of the old man on the Toyoko Line—had no aura of power. They were unhealthily white, freckled and short, without bulges or throbbing, subcutaneous veins. His hands, short-fingered and liver-spotted, had fine lines of grit that even Papa's industrial-strength hand soap couldn't remove. And his left thumbnail, split lengthwise when he'd dropped a chunk of steel on it long ago, had never grown back together. The cuticle had invaded the crack, erupting out of the nail in a narrow V, below which the crack itself had darkened to a thick brown line. When his hands worked, the arms came to life—not in swellings but in hard channels and subtle shadows that writhed in unison beneath the skin and suggested the patient, inexhaustible strength that comes from using the human body like an old tool, well-balanced and simply crafted.

These two rather unexpected stimuli, the old man and the memory of Papa, led me circuitously to sumo, because it struck me then that most sumo wrestlers don't have athletes' arms. They have Papa's arms.

Athletes' arms today are splendid hybrids—like high-yield feed corn—dense, boneless, beautiful—heavy with knots of unnatural power, kneaded and nurtured into contours of Hellenic perfection with barbells and drills, chrome-plated machinery, physics, nutrition, chemistry. Athletes' arms are the cosmetic handiwork of sport, sculpted for tank-top nakedness . . . massive, rippling, blue-veined and awe-inspiring.

Now, set aside a couple of notable exceptions, and you cannot find a rikishi whose arms fit that description—because sumo wrestlers don't work like that. While most athletes' arms are—to a significant degree—the products of vanity, rikishi are a Luddite remnant who smith the tool of their trade, their flesh, in drudgery. Like Papa.

Like that stringy old husk on the train.

Rikishi have arms and legs and shoulders not like linebackers, gymnasts and swimmers, but like railroaders and stevedores and icemen. Their regimen is tedious and two-dimensional; their weight-training is medieval; their strength grows haphazardly in a mindless cycle of grubby, stumbling practice matches; their conditioning is regressive, and their diet is bilious. And they're grossly underpaid. In all these respects, they are out of tune with modern athletic science. The trials of their flesh connect them more intimately with working people—with their audience in the pit, whose daily struggle is equally tedious, two-dimensional, grubby, stumbling, regressive, bilious and underpaid—than all their athletic contemporaries.

Sumo wrestlers' arms, legs, shoulders, backs are ordinary—like the withered claw of that old railroad worker. And we see ourselves in that ordinary flesh. We sense the weakness there, but we know—because most of us have a Papa of our own—the quiet force that hides within.

But listen. Sumo's allure doesn't just come from this sort of male bonding in the ordeals of the flesh, but also in its feminine manifestation. In its beauty.

Beauty?

All right, this is something that women had to explain to me. Not every sumo fan is a closet Machinist. Women laugh when I speak of "unsightly fat" on men. In the sumo ring's nudity, women perceive softness, smoothness, sensuality, a huge, hairless, silky, breathing form upon which one can creep and climb, explore, taste and smell and probe and play out a whole anthology of larger-than-life sexual imaginings.

After a few women explained sumo thus—as a vicarious bout of sensual frolic—it gradually began to register. Yes, I nodded reluctantly, there is something in the epic surfeit of sumo blubber, in its antic movement—bouncing, wiggling, sliding, shivering, drooping in fold upon fold down the rikishi's body and bulging out between the plump fingers of his clutching opponent—that inspires a desire to reach out and touch, explore its feel, play with it like armfuls of warm Jell-O. Thus freed from my subconscious fetters, I remembered a fragment of Moby Dick—Melville's most erotic passage—conceived in a setting, the whaling ship, where there are only men, physically intimate because their work presses them together. Like on the dohyo.

"Squeeze! squeeze! squeeze! all the morning long; I squeezed that sperm till I myself almost melted into it; I squeezed that sperm till a strange sort of insanity came over me; and I found myself unwittingly squeezing my co-laborers' hands in it, mistaking their hands for the gentle globules. Such an abounding, affectionate, friendly, loving feeling did this avocation beget; that at last I was continually squeezing their hands, and looking up into their eyes sentimentally; as much to say, — Oh! my dear fellow beings, why should we longer cherish any social acerbities, or know the slightest ill-humor or envy! Come; let us squeeze hands all around; nay, let us all squeeze ourselves into each other; let us squeeze ourselves universally into the very milk and sperm of kindness.

"Would that I could keep squeezing that sperm for ever!"*

You see, women explained to me, sumo wrestlers give rise to that desire to fondle. Other jocks can't bring it off. Some athletes are as naked as rikishi, but they're not squeezable. Some are squeezable, but not naked. Only rikishi waddle into our hearts, shimmy sentimentally and whisper, from the folds of their ample flesh, "Let us all squeeze ourselves into each other . . . "

The Way of All Flesh
Love, work, and fat. We sumo fans develop our passion a little older and a little deeper than for other sports because of these three sumo characteristics.

*Melville, Herman, *Moby Dick*, Penguin Classics, London, 1986: p. 527.

We have not enough of the first, and too damn much of the latter two.

Sumo radiates a metaphor of life, our flesh, our naked vulnerability, our self-delusions. As we learn the ordeal of the rikishi's life, we see men who are forced, by their profession's regimen, to undergo an accelerated ageing process. The thirty-year-old sumo wrestler has the joints, intestines, heart, and arteries of a man twenty years older—if he's lucky. His path to retirement is a race against total decrepitude. He connives to save some of his strength and vitality to use after the end of his career, so that he might get some use from the years remaining to him, and recover from the abuse he has inflicted on his flesh in his effort to make a living.

You don't need to be a sumo wrestler to recognize that feeling.

It shouldn't be like this. Our work shouldn't vitiate our bodies and fill us with a desperation to escape. Sumo fans understand what's happening, and their enthusiasm for the sport is certainly, in part, a sympathy for that involuntary corrosion that becomes the way of all workaday flesh. And the rikishi, dumb as they look, understand what's being done to them.

Kitao/Futahaguro said that, above all sumo's other flaws, he deplores the incompetence of physical training, nutrition and medical care in the sport. "You can be big, even fat, but to have a body that is really healthy, safe against injury, you need certain types of food, more scientific practice methods, weight training," he said. "I did these things for myself, but not every rikishi has that discipline . . . "

If we all applied science and nutrition and discipline to our lives, the abuses of working life wouldn't be so deadly. But it's a rare human—as Kitao/Futahaguro and his former colleagues in sumo demonstrate—whose discipline is so steady. Most of us tumble off the wagon now and then. And those who don't, the ones who drive the wagon—like the rare, brilliant, robotlike athletes who never sweat, never cuss and retire seemingly at the peak of their power—repel us somehow with the shallowness of their humanity. The grind—even if we're good at it—wears us out by and by, and we resent the imperturbable paragon whose faltering flesh never seems to foreshadow the inevitable collapse.

Rikishi are naked. No armor to hide their sweat, their lumps, their fear, their decay. Rikishi, fed with slow poison and forced to grow old even faster than we do, rarely offend us with their perfection. Their flesh is our flesh, their nakedness our exposure, their decay our decay. What they do, how they live, what they fear, is the same that we do and live and fear—but bigger, faster, scarier.

In sumo, we feel the ordinariness of these men, their mediocrity. Most of them retire as losers. And simultaneously, in sumo, we enjoy the grotesque that is the alter ego of its ordinariness. We see what would happen if, instead of battling with balky Xerox machines and pointless memos from idiot managers, we could take a swing at someone else, anyone, wrestle another human being to the dirt and release all that pent-up frustration. A grotesque image—real people naked, clawing at each other's fat and smacking each other's faces, squeezing one another into gasping submission.

But we can imagine it—easily. We can wish it!

In sumo, we see what would happen if we—

ordinary people—just said to hell with all the self-restraint, the diet and the budget and the vanity, and just pigged out, every day, swelling into a monstrous, lolling, comfortable decadence. Oh, to be fat and flagrant, admired for the very indolent obesity that should horrify and ostracize us.

Weird, but we can imagine it—easily. And we can—in weary, hungry, lazy moments—wish it!

The hitch (there's always a hitch) in the wishful thinking is in the nudge of reality. If we got into such a state, we probably couldn't move from the spot. You've heard the one about the press agent who excitedly tells the burlesque theater manager about his new act—a gorgeous girl with a 60-inch bust.

His eyes lighting up, the theater manager says, "Wow! What does she do?"

"Well, with a little help she can sit up . . . "

And therein lies another secret of sumo's fleshly pleasure, because rikishi—even the most bizarre and distended, even Konishiki—can sit up without help. They stand, they move, they keep their balance, and they kick ass. They express, in their daily battles, a stubborn faith that lurks in the backs of all our minds . . .

"All right," this little voice whispers to us, "I'm older than I was, and yeah, I've put on a few pounds. Maybe I've lost a step or two. A little past my prime. But goddammit, I know a few tricks these young punks haven't even heard of yet. I'm tougher than I look. I can still do it."

The voice begets empathy. We can identify with the prematurely old young men of sumo more sincerely than Olympic Adonises and the Myrmidons of pro football. We admire, often, not how well they can fight, but that they can fight at all. And we even tolerate the connivance of sumo, yaochozumo, because we concede them all the help they can get. And besides, why should sumo be different from anything else in life? Doesn't everybody cut a few corners?

As I was finishing this book, Mike Royko reminded his readers that even baseball, the American sacrament, tolerates its own undercurrent of yaocho—pervasive, unmentioned and tolerated to the very highest level. "Part of the tradition of baseball is cheating," said Royko in one of his Chicago *Tribune* dialogs with himself.

"... How can I say that? What about the spitball? That's cheating, but the announcers laugh and say what a sly guy the pitcher is for getting away with it. Or the Vaseline ball. Or when the pitcher hides sandpaper in his glove. Everybody says, 'Wow, what a cagey character.' Or when a guy is tagged out, but the umpire blows it. Does the guy stand up like a man and say: 'Umpire, I must be truthful. I was out.' Of course he don't. Is that honest? It's like getting extra dough in change in a store and not giving it back. It ain't exactly stealing, but it's cheating. So cheating goes on all the time in baseball."*

Yaocho in sumo, yaocho in Yankee Stadium, it is a flaw in the fabric of the sport that we wish was not there, but we accept it, even admire it, because the players are flawed like us—and clever like us! They

*Royko, Mike, copyright 1990, by the Chicago *Tribune*.

might not cheat if they really had control of their own sport, but it's part of the system, and they can't change the system, not without getting in big trouble, just like us...

. . . the way of all flesh.

The feel of sumo is, I think, closer than any other sport to how we feel, or perhaps how we would feel if we could re-make ourselves as stars. The players are fat and slow, hurt and tired, yet grand and mighty above it all. And above it all, sensual . . . desirable. Lovable.

Kitao/Futahaguro again: "The process before tachiai is the best part! You can see their skin color change, as they become more and more excited. Their bodies harden, grow more and more tense . . . "

The Final Touch

The rikishi, in his vulnerable nudity, his unsubtle sensualism, his fragile humanity, struggles for all of us, summons our feelings into that sandy circle. This is what is so extraordinarily engaging in sumo, but not—at last—what keeps people coming back to the pit. It needs one more ingredient.

People still gotta have heroes. Rikishi must be like all of us—the troubled flesh, the anxious waiting, the frustrating defeat—but the best of them must still be better than we could ever dream of being. Sumo thrives on the backs of its true athletes, the ones with epic bodies, acrobatic quickness, steel will and penetrating intellects. Sumo thrives because the very best win without need of yaocho, because the sport's finest moments radiate excellence and remain resolutely pure.

The great rikishi beat the fat ones; they beat the

cheaters and they beat the system. The way to the top is still the way Kirishima took in 1989. He worked harder than he had ever worked, changed his diet, lifted weights every day instead of napping, sought practice matches against his most formidable foes and disciplined his mind to take every challenge one day at a time. He followed the same pattern that we would recognize in the habits of Franz Beckenbauer, Nolan Ryan or Larry Bird.

It's a strange blend. No other sport presents daily bouts between the superb and the ridiculous, Dolph Lundgren versus Ralph Cramden. No other professional sport so naturally balances our intimations of mortality against our search for gods.

I thought of summarizing sumo here by cataloguing all those elements of the sport that could be improved, including the lurking presence of yaocho. I thought of laying out a program that would relax the relentless schedule, cut down on travel and practice and give each rikishi at least one basho off every year. I was going to suggest means to introduce science to sumo—nutrition, Nautilus machines, sports medicine, testosterone injections—which would eventually weed out the Butterballs and Cabdrivers, creating a new master race of cookie-cutter hunks, like the Soviet gymnastics squad or the lineup of finalists in the Mr. Olympia pageant.

But all sumo's problems are obvious to the alert fan, and they are matters that come under the heading of "What's the use?" Sumo fans, cherishing the sport's traditions and knowing its blemishes, hover perpetually between conservatism and reformism. However, the Sumo Association suffers no such ambivalence. The old farts will continue—without a second thought—their comfortable habits of brain-washing, hazing, ostracism, flagrant nepotism, and favoring Hippos over all other aspirants. There is selfishness, injustice, tyranny in sumo, and I've bridled at them all, and I'll do it again—out loud, with you if you want. But it's all recreational bitching, and I can't keep it up, because there are bigger problems elsewhere in the world.

Sumo is what it is, and it will remain just so, impervious and dependable—like an old friend, like your first sex, like that first wonderful sentence of *The Catcher in the Rye*. After the bitching, sumo remains more fun than hassle. It will always invite you—hey, seduce you—to fog your eyes and feel yourself hugging Kotogaume's epic boobs, steering Kirinishiki's world-class love-handles, admiring the sensuous curve of Sakahoko's tummy, grinding thighs with Baby Huey, busting Takatoriki's nasty chops, rolling in the dirt with Akinoshima, sharing the frenzy of Kasugafuji's werewolf charge, or aching spitefully to grab a chair-leg and knock that shit-eating grin off Mitoizumi's face!

Sumo lets you put yourself there, feel yourself on the dohyo—because it's the way you would fight, one-on-one, overweight and awkward. Sumo touches us—well, at least one of us— because the fat guys are more human, more oppressed, more bewildered by it all than almost all the strobe-lit hotshots of our time. But meanwhile, they are, like all athletes, our heroic stand-ins. They serve, bare-assed and nervous, in our place—just like us . . . only more so.

It takes a while to absorb the nuances of sumo, and to disregard its distractions. It takes longer to tolerate its deficiencies. But if you give yourself that time, accept those flaws, and allow yourself the empathy that rikishi irresistibly inspire, then, by and by, you will find yourself in tune, and moving with the beat; and shouting the very same Orwellian cry that echoes from two eager throats in our little living room 90 days a year . . .

"Come on, Lardass! Rip that pig's face off!"

EPILOGUE
The End of History

While I was putting the finishing touches on this book, Chiyonofuji retired and sumo history ended. It was a clumsy and ignominious departure that besmirched—but only slightly—Chiyo's career.

Chiyonofuji foreshadowed his failure in the May Basho of 1991 by deciding beforehand to just "see how it goes." This halfhearted approach was uncharacteristic of Chiyonofuji—almost as if he'd looked at a girl in the bleachers in the last seconds before tachiai. After so egregiously compromising his concentration, Chiyonofuji had a first-day match against the leader of the Fujishima-beya Brat Pack, Takahanada (Little Spoon). Even when the other rikishi is ready for him, wrestling Little Spoon is like carrying a potted tree up a stairwell. Chiyonofuji, distracted by thoughts of retirement, wasn't ready. He lost, falling backward off the dohyo while the kid dove at his feet.

Two days later, Chiyo lost again to another Brat Packer, Takatoriki (Dangerous Dan), and that was enough for him. Chiyo quit the business and granted the obligatory default to Misugisato on Day 4, his last official scheduled match. He made his announcement, wept manfully, and answered questions about sumo's teen dream, Takahanada.

This was appropriate because it was the loss to Little Spoon that "ended history," that told Chiyo he didn't care enough anymore about pushing children around on the sand. Those three days in May marked dramatic changes in the complexion of sumo. Among the repercussions:

• Kokonoe-beya, which Chiyo (under his new name, Jimmaku) will eventually inherit from coach Kokonoe, ceased instantly to be sumo's most prominent stable. Chiyo's departure left behind in the makuuchi division only a borderline psycho (Hokutoumi), a fading fish (Takanofuji) and a green Butterball (Tomoefuji). This is middle-of-the-pack material.

• Fujishima and his Brat Pack went immediately to the head of the class, with the enthusiastic blessing of Uncle Futagoyama and the Sumo Association. The Brat Pack is the vanguard of a Sumo Association "youth movement" that, in 1990–91, brutally pushed aside some of sumo's most likeable veterans. With five rikishi now in makuuchi—Big Spoon, Little Spoon, Dangerous Dan, Akinoshima and Frankenstein—Fujishima-beya has, in the upper ranks, a logjam of its own wrestlers who never have to oppose one another. This is the stuff of dynasties. Barring injuries, Fujishima-beya seems certain for at least one yokozuna promotion in the early '90s, and a flock of pretty easy tournament trophies. This, alas, won't be especially pretty, because none of the Brat Pack is close, yet, to becoming a polished wrestler.

• Other sumobeya will struggle to forestall the Fujishima monopoly, but with only sporadic success. The best opposition is either getting old (Asahifuji, Hokutoumi, Konishiki, and Kirishima) or they're as raw as the Brat Pack. Among the promising young challengers are Akebono (the Great Pumpkin), Daishoyama (Dimples), Kotonowaka, Daishoho and (a very dark, but delightful, horse) Mainoumi (Mighty Mouse).

• Sumo, in general, will languish in a period of transition in which Chiyonofuji—and his superb repertoire of moves—will be conspicuously absent. Chiyonofuji spoiled a generation of sumo fans. The only hints of Chiyo's heritage will be Asahifuji's moments of extraordinary agility, and Kirishima's astounding strength and occasional bursts of inspired technique.

Otherwise, sumo will be dominated by athletic novices like Takahanada, unmanageable behemoths like Akebono, and eye-gouging bullies like Takatoriki.

Well, that sounds like fun, too, though, doesn't it?

It will be. And it will be even more fun when, inevitably—from who knows where?—another once-in-a-lifetime rikishi, Chiyo's heir, will quietly show up. He will uplift the entire strange sport, force it to compete at his level and lend fresh dignity to the daily parade of slapstick and blubber.

GLOSSARY

Although this book is distinctly not a comprehensive guide to sumo terminology (especially of the dumber variety), I was forced to include a number of actual Japanese words as I wrote it. In order to help the reader cope with this imposition, these terms are compiled and defined—after a fashion—below.

ankogata: A sumo body-type that suggests athleticism.

banzuke: The Sumo Association's bi-monthly roster of rankings.

basho: A sumo tournament, 15 days in length.

chankonabe: The main diet of sumo wrestlers; a cholesterol cocktail.

dohyō: The raised sand and mud platform on which the fat guys wrestle.

fundoshi: A Japanese jock strap.

gaijin: A foreigner in Japan.

gakusei-zumō: An educated sumo wrestler.

genki: Fit as a fiddle and ready for love.

geta: Wooden platform shoes.

goombai: The referee's lacquered "war fan," which he points in the direction of the winner's corner to show the outcome of a match.

gyōji: The referee; an ugly cheerleader; human costume jewelry.

hataki: A form of boxing in sumo, with blows directed mainly at the opponent's face and head.

hataki-komi: The "matador" move, in which one wrestler leaps aside to avoid his opponent's charge, then pushes his opponent down as he charges by.

hidari-uwate: Sumo jargon.

hidari-yotsu: A lefthand belt grip.

jūryō: The second of the three broad rankings of sumo wrestlers; between *makuuchi* and *makushita*.

kachikoshi: A majority of wins (at least eight) in a 15-day tournament; insurance against demotion in the ranks.

komusubi: The fourth highest individual rank in sumo and the lowest of the four *sanyaku* ranks; the borderline between the exalted stars and the rank-and-file.

maegashira: The lowest, and largest, category of individual sumo ranks in the upper *(makuuchi)* division; the rank-and-file fat guys.

makekoshi: A minority of wins (seven or fewer) in a 15-day tournament; after this, you get demoted in the ranks.

makushita: The lowest of the three broad rankings of sumo wrestlers; below *makuuchi* and *jūryō*.

makuuchi: The highest of the three broad rankings of sumo wrestlers; above *juryo* and *makushita*.

mawashi: The sumo wrestler's belt, or sash.

migi-yotsu: A righthand belt grip.

mono ii: Review of a referee's call by the panel of judges.

morozashi: Both hands on the other fat guy's belt; the death grip.

obāsan/obaasan: Granny.

obentō: Box lunch.

obi: A belt for a *yukata*, necessary because *yukata* don't have buttons down the front.

ojii-san: Gramps.

omiyage: An obligatory gift.

oshibori: Washcloth.

oshidashi: Victory by pushing.

oyakata: The master and coach of a sumo stable, formerly a wrestler himself.

ōzeki: The second highest individual rank in sumo, just below *yokozuna*.

rikishi: The best term for sumo wrestler; "big strong bastard."

sagari: A silly fringe that hangs down from a sumo wrestler's belt.

sanyaku: The top four individual ranks in sumo's upper division—including *yokozuna*, *ōzeki*, *sekiwake*, and *komusubi*.

sekitori: A term for sumo wrestler; equivalent to *rikishi* and *sumotōri*.

sekiwake: The third highest individual rank in sumo, below *yokozuna* and *ōzeki*.

shikō: Foot-stomping.

shita: Below.

somebody no Kachi: The victory announcement, in which "somebody" is replaced by the winner's name and "*kachi*" means he "won."

something-dashi: Any winning move that involves pushing.

something-tenage: Any winning move that involves an arm throw.

soppugata: A sumo body type that suggests flab.

sumōbeya: A sumo stable; Japan's version of "Animal House."

sumōtori: Another term for sumo wrestler.

tabi: Japanese socks.

tachiai: The face-off and collision that begins each sumo match.

tawara: The circle of sand-packed rice-straw bales within which the fat guys wrestle; cross the *tawara* first and you lose.

tsunatori: Promotion of a sumo wrestler from *ozeki,* the second highest rank, to *yokozuna,* the highest rank.

tsuppari: A form of boxing in sumo, with blows directed mainly at the opponent's neck and chest.

tsuridashi: Victory by carrying the opponent off the *dohyo;* the Big Hernia.

uchigake: Gobbledegook.

utchari: Victory by last-second reversal of positions.

uwa: Above.

yakitori: Barbecued food on sticks, usually chicken, or chicken entrails, or parts of the chicken that make entrails, by comparison, seem appetizing.

yaocho-zumō: An arranged match; a tank job; a dive.

yokozuna: The highest individual sumo ranking; superstar.

yorikiri: Victory by grabbing the belt with two hands, lifting, grunting and pushing; the missionary position.

yukata: A cotton bathrobe; the sumo wrestler's daily attire.

yūshō: The championship of a 15-day tournament.

zōri: Dress sandals.

Other Titles in the Tuttle Library of Martial Arts

AIKIDO AND THE DYNAMIC SPHERE
by Adele Westbrook and Oscar Ratti

Aikido is a Japanese method of self-defense that can be used against any form of attack and that is also a way of harmonizing all of one's vital powers into an integrated, energy-filled whole.

BLACK BELT KARATE *by Jordan Roth*

A no-frills, no-holds barred handbook on the fundamentals of modern karate. Over 800 techniques and exercises and more than 1,850 photographs reveal the speed and power inherent in properly taught karate.

THE ESSENCE OF OKINAWAN KARATE-DO
by Shoshin Nagamine

"Nagamine's book will awaken in all who read it a new understanding of the Okinawan open-handed martial art."

—Gordon Warner
Kendo 7th dan, renshi

THE NINJA AND THEIR SECRET FIGHTING ART
by Stephen K. Hayes

The *ninja* were the elusive spies and assassins of feudal Japan. This book explains their lethal system of unarmed combat, unique weapons, and mysterious techniques of stealth.

SECRET FIGHTING ARTS OF THE WORLD
by John F. Gilbey

Suppressed for centuries, twenty of the world's most secretly guarded fighting techniques are vividly described in this amazing volume.

SECRETS OF THE SAMURAI *by Oscar Ratti and Adele Westbrook*

A definitive study of the martial arts of feudal Japan, illustrating the techniques, weapons, strategies, and principles of combat that made the Japanese samurai a terrible foe.

JUDO FORMAL TECHNIQUES *by Tadao Otaki and Donn F. Draeger*

A comprehensive manual on the basic formal techniques of Kodokan Judo, the Randori no Kata, which provide the fundamental training in throwing and grappling that is essential to effective Judo.

THIS IS KENDO *by Junzo Sasamori and Gordon Warner*

The first book in English to describe the origin and history of kendo, its basic principles and techniques, its etiquette, and its relation to Zen. A must for any serious martial artist.

THE WAY OF KARATE *by George E. Mattson*

A fully illustrated explanation of the Okinawan style of karate; an indispensable introduction to its true nature and basic techniques, with emphasis on its value in both training and self-defense.